S0-BOI-518

101
Things To Do
In The Year
2000

101

Things To Do
In The Year
2000

Dan Penwell

Tulsa, Oklahoma

2nd Printing

Scripture quotations marked KJV are taken from the *King James Version* of the Bible.

Scripture quotations marked NIV are taken from the *Holy Bible, New International Version* ®. NIV ®. Copyright © 1973, 1978, 1984 by International Bible Society. Used by permission of Zondervan Publishing House. All rights reserved.

GOD'S WORD is a copyrighted work of God's Word to the Nations Bible Society. Quotations are used by permission. Copyright 1995 by God's Word to the Nations Bible Society. All rights reserved.

101 Things To Do In The Year 2000
ISBN   1-56292-802-3
Copyright ©1999 by GRQ Ink, Inc.
381 Riverside Drive, Suite #250
Franklin, TN   37064

Published by Honor Books
P.O. Box 55388
Tulsa, OK 74155

Developed by GRQ Ink, Inc.
Designed by Richmond & Williams
Composition by John Reinhardt Book Design

Manuscript written by Dan Penwell

Printed in the United States of America. All rights reserved under International Copyright Law. Contents and/or cover may not be reproduced in whole or in part in any form without the express written consent of the Publisher.

ACKNOWLEDGMENTS

My appreciation goes to Honor Books and to their president and my friend, Keith Provance, for recognizing the book's potential.

And to my wife, Gloria, who spent many evenings and weekends alone before I finally retired, thank you for your patience and understanding. I love you.

Thanks to my children, Derek, Daren, Darcey, and Dana, who often called with the perennial question, "How's the book coming?"

And a special thanks to my mother, who has always encouraged me but asked the same perennial question, "How's the book coming?"

Finally, I thank the Lord, who loves me even when I'm unlovable and has given me the opportunity to share with others some of my feelings and convictions.

Dan Penwell

INTRODUCTION

WHY YOU SHOULD READ THIS BOOK

Three of the most challenging, yet moving, words that a child will ever hear from his or her peers are, "I dare you." The dare could be as simple as jumping across a large mud puddle or as embarrassing as kissing for the first time. A dare, for some reason, creates the impetus to try something new, so consider this book to contain 101 "I dare you's" for the year 2000.

Dale Carnegie declared, "The man who goes farthest is generally the one who is willing to do and dare. The sure-thing boat never gets far from shore." Hopefully, this book will provide the spark and be the catalyst for you to find a more fulfilling, exciting, and meaningful purpose in life.

Why have I compiled *101 Things To Do In The Year 2000*? All of us need to be stretched beyond the comfortable and complacent, or as the bumper sticker says, "The only difference between a rut and a grave is the depth." Accept the challenge to get out of the rut, to do something new and different, to make a difference in your life and your family's life, and to make this first year of the new millennium your most meaningful and memorable year ever.

I dare you!

CONTENTS

That man is a success who has lived well,
Laughed often and loved much;
Who has gained the respect of intelligent
    men and the love of children;
Who has filled his niche and accom-
    plished his task;
Who leaves the world better than he
    found it,
Whether by a perfect poem or a rescued
    soul;
Who never lacked appreciation of earth's
    beauty or failed to express it;
Who looked for the best in others and
    gave the best he had.

—Robert Louis Stevenson

101 Things To Do In The Year **2000**

PLANT A TREE FOR YOUR CHILDREN OR GRANDCHILDREN

"I think that I shall never
see a poem lovely as a tree."

—Joyce Kilmer

Any idea how many trees the average person consumes during a lifetime? With all the wooden structures, furniture, computer printouts, books, and newspapers, the average person would be aghast if he or she knew how many trees it takes to live today.

One marvelous gesture you can make as you enter into the new millennium is to plant a tree for each of your children or grandchildren. Dedicate each tree in the name of one specific child. You might select a tree that has characteristics that remind you of that child—an oak tree for a strong, solid boy; a purple plum for a delicate, beautiful girl; a pine tree for that child who loves the holiday seasons; a palm tree for the one who is filled with rhythm.

Make or purchase a plaque that commemorates each child and each tree. The plaque could say something as simple as, "Dedicated to Nicole Johnson, Born 1991." Since the tree will likely be too small to attach a plaque, give the plaque to the child to place on the tree as it grows in the years ahead.

 Interestingly, in both the second chapter of Genesis and the last chapter of Revelation in the Bible, trees play a prominent role. Genesis 2 mentions the Tree of the Knowledge of Good and Evil, and Revelation 22 depicts the Tree of Life.

101 Things To Do In The Year 2000

FAST FOR A DAY

"I (Ezra) proclaimed a fast, so that we might humble ourselves before our God and ask him for a safe journey for us and our children, with all our possessions. . . . So we fasted and petitioned our God about this, and he answered our prayer."

—Ezra 8:21-23 NIV

Fasting. Has that become the latest diet gimmick for losing weight? Is it an empty religious formality? Or is there spiritual value in fasting?

A definition of fasting includes the practice of abstaining from food for a specific period of time as a spiritual discipline; a method of concentrating and riveting one's attention upon God through prayer and meditation.

Fasting is referred to and practiced throughout the Old and New Testaments. The Jews have observed it in connection with the Day of Atonement, Yom Kippur, and as a form of penitence and purification. Jesus not only spoke positively about it in the Sermon on the Mount—He Himself practiced fasting for forty days at the start of His ministry. The early Christians fasted and prayed as they sought direction from God, and the tradition has continued throughout the past twenty centuries.

As you begin a new millennium, fasting could well be the springboard for refocusing your life beyond your own wants and needs. It may be the means of resolving the spiritual direction your life should take. As you enter into year 2000, commit one full day to fasting. Use this day to reflect and pray and listen, determining God's will for your life.

FYI

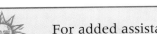

For added assistance, read a copy of *Fasting for Spiritual Breakthrough* by Elmer Towns.

CREATE A YEAR 2000 SCRAPBOOK

"The world does not need so much to be informed as to be reminded."

—Sir Thomas More

The year 2000! Who would have thought it? Men have been predicting the end of the world for centuries. Some are even predicting that the world will end in the year 2000, and the concern over the Y2K bug has been an additional prod.

But the year 2000 is now a reality. You can make it a year to remember by chronicling 2000 with a scrapbook. Arrange your scrapbook to highlight both family and historical events.

First some ground rules:

- Involve the whole family. This is to be everyone's project—not just mom's.
- Develop a game plan together. Decide whether the scrapbook will be set up chronologically, topically, or by family member.
- Purchase a quality scrapbook and supplies, readily available at stationery and office supply stores.

What do you include? Whatever you like, but here are a few suggestions. Include souvenirs of the year 2000 celebrations, school papers, newspaper articles, letters and cards, photographs, remembrances from your church, vacation memorabilia, and a wide variety of mementos and keepsakes that will come your way.

Most of all, have fun creating your scrapbook together.

For added assistance contact *Creating Keepsakes Scrapbook Magazine* at 888-247-5282. A good Web site resource is www.scrapbooksupplies.com.

101 Things To Do In The Year **2000**

LIST YOUR LIFE'S 100 MOST IMPORTANT EVENTS

> "Restlessness is discontent—and discontent is the first necessity of progress. Show me a thoroughly satisfied man and I will show you a failure."
>
> —Thomas Alva Edison

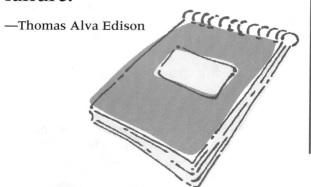

For many years, the ideas of contemplation, review, and critique have been frightening concepts. The French philosopher René Descartes gave the following advice, "Learn less and contemplate more." This admonition is as important today as it was when first given more than three hundred years ago.

In the 1960s, Ralph Edwards hosted a TV show entitled *This Is Your Life*. It normally involved a well-known personality who, under some noble pretense, was the honored guest for the TV show. Family, friends, and acquaintances were introduced as the means of remembering important episodes of past years. Even though the initial surprise was embarrassing, the reflection and review of life's important events proved exhilarating, exciting, satisfying, and motivating.

As you enter into the new millennium, it's a great time to look back. Make the year 2000 the year for personal reflection and draw up a list of the 100 most important events in your life, so far.

Here are some ideas.

- Get away by yourself in a quiet place for half a day—someplace like the woods or library.

- Review events year by year, then write down on a pad those that impacted your life.

- See if you can come up with 100 important events that have shaped who you are.

THE NEXT STEP

This also might be a good time to review your spiritual journey.

ORGANIZE YOUR OLD PHOTOS

> "Not everybody trusts paintings, but people believe photographs."
>
> —Ansel Adams

Most households have at least one person who loves to take pictures—pictures of family, friends, pets, vacations, and special events. But half the fun of taking pictures is viewing the results. Maybe you've heard something like, "Mom, do you know where those pictures are that we took at Walt Disney World?" or "Dad, whatever happened to the photos of our Little League team?" This longing to view the photos of a group or an event is one of the great anticipations of modern life. It might run a close second to anticipating the opening of packages on Christmas morning.

Let's fast-forward a year or five years or ten years. Listen to this updated public service announcement: "Parents, do you know where your accumulated family pictures are?" How will you answer? "They are in the big box in the hall closet" or "I think they are in one of the drawers in the spare bedroom"?

As you begin a new millennium, why not make organizing your photographs a primary goal for the year 2000? A very recent trend is to organize your photos through the use of computer software such as *FlipAlbum*. Whatever means you use, be certain to have a well-developed plan. Decide before starting whether it will be organized by specific dates, by year, by event, or by personality.

THE NEXT STEP

Whether you have children at home or ones who are grown, share with them your goal of organizing all your photos in some type of album. Without a doubt, they will want to be involved and see the results.

SIGN UP FOR AN ADULT EDUCATION COURSE

"There is a time in
every man's
education
when he arrives
at the conviction
that envy is
ignorance; that
imitation is
suicide."

—Ralph Waldo Emerson

Have you ever wished you were a gourmet cook? Does the computer scare you? Do you know the difference between a stock, a bond, and a mutual fund? Did you ever want to learn about electricity, auto mechanics, upholstery, or bread baking? Does running your own business have strong appeal? How about building your own house?

Opportunities to learn these skills and hundreds of others are readily available through your community adult education courses, and they are inexpensive. Besides learning a new skill or trade, such a class is a wonderful place to make new friends. It affords the opportunity to network with others, and this could prove beneficial in your current job. It is also exhilarating and will give you a new lease on life.

Make the year 2000 the year that you increase your knowledge. If you have been a couch potato in recent times, resolve that this is the year you are going to change—you are going to learn something new and exciting. Check your local community education centers to see when the next classes start. Have them put your name on the mailing list and ask for a current catalog.

FINAL THOUGHT

As you enter the year 2000, don't be satisfied with the status quo when life-changing opportunities are readily available.

101 Things To Do In The Year 2000

GET SET UP ON THE INTERNET

> "As a general rule, the most successful man in life is the man who has the best information."

—Benjamin Disraeli

The electronic information highway affords you one of the great inventions and conveniences in the history of humankind. Through a computer in your home, the wealth of knowledge at the public library, and possibly even more, is at your fingertips. The person who is not connected to the world through the Internet is being left behind when it comes to information, data, and entertainment.

Do you want to check the latest ball scores? How about finding a recipe? Or ordering your groceries? Do you need factual information on a new or used car before you buy it? How are your investments doing this very minute on the stock market? What factors should you consider before refinancing your house? Can you find and order the newest book by your favorite author? Yes, yes, yes to all these questions—and you can even chat and debate with others over the plight of our political leaders or the existence of God. Anything that you can imagine may be accessed through the Internet.

Some useful sites on the Internet: www.yahoo.com, www.consumerworld.org, www.worldnetdaily.com, www.home.miningco.com, and www.travelocity.com.

PHONE ONE OF YOUR SCHOOL
OR COLLEGE FRIENDS

"True friendship is like sound health; the value of it is seldom known until it be lost."

—Charles Caleb Colton

Some of life's most memorable and enjoyable times are the good old school days. There were the parties . . . bizarre teachers . . . food fights . . . championship games . . . school plays . . . practical jokes . . . all-night study sessions . . . skipping classes . . . homecoming . . . and of course, graduation day. It's fun to reminisce about those days, but what made them special was not just the school, the activities, or the teachers—it was the close friendships that were formed.

As a new millennium dawns, why not use that turning point as the reason to renew some of those old friendships? Imagine the pleasure and joy you'd experience if one of your former friends were to call you unexpectedly some evening. Both you and the friend making the call would enjoy the delight of the moment.

Sometime during the year 2000, take the initiative to make that telephone call yourself. Of those three or four close friends, which ones have you not talked to since school? By doing a little checking on the Internet or through telephone information, you should be able to come up with their telephone numbers.

Much of life comes and goes but friends are forever.

Two great resources for finding people on the Internet are www.555-1212.com and www.theultimates.com/white.

MAKE PLANS TO TAKE YOUR DREAM VACATION

"Vacations are a little like love—anticipated with relish, experienced with inconvenience, and remembered with nostalgia."

—Anonymous

Have you always wanted to go to Paris or Rome? Are the cruise lines urging you to take that trip to the Caribbean that you've been wanting for so long? Perhaps you'd pick Australia or Hawaii.

Vacations are refreshing, but all the good intentions in the world are simply good intentions if there are no plans. It doesn't do any harm to dream, providing you get up and hustle when the alarm goes off.

Whether you've already chosen your vacation or are still only dreaming, the best place to begin planning is a travel agency. Colorful circulars on every fun and exciting place in the world are readily available at no cost. These brochures make dreaming even more fun and will help you plot your trip. A travel agent is there to help you plan as well as to provide an estimated cost of your vacation package. As you know, half the fun of going on a vacation is the planning and anticipation.

Other great resources are the public library, video stores, travel magazines, and the travel section in your local bookstore. The Internet provides an overabundance of travel resources and information.

Let the words of the late George Bernard Shaw in *Back to Methuselah* be your byline: "You see things; and you say, 'Why?' But I dream things that never were; and I say 'Why not?'"

THE NEXT STEP

 Do more than fantasize—make actual plans for that dream vacation in the year 2000.

101 Things To Do In The Year 2000

MAKE COOKIES FOR YOUR NEXT-DOOR NEIGHBORS

"People don't care how much you know until they know how much you care."

—Anonymous

John and Mary Hopkins had "new" neighbors on their left who had moved in two years ago. The families waved at each other on occasion and even spoke politely, but John and Mary had never taken the initiative to get to know these new neighbors. The Hopkinses had good intentions, but that's all. Their neighbors on the right were longtime residents when the Hopkinses moved in. They always seemed friendly, but no reciprocal relationship had been built other than an occasional nod. Recently, a new family moved in across the street, and the Hopkinses still have not learned their names.

This story is fictitious, but it conveys the biting reality that we tend to live in our own little private worlds.

How about you? Do you know your neighbors? Do you consider yourself a good neighbor? Do you offer information or help when they may need it?

As a new millennium dawns, why not make it your goal to become a caring neighbor? Plan to set aside one evening and make a huge batch of cookies. Then, with an appropriate neighborly greeting card or written note, deliver the cookies as a family. Let your neighbors know that you truly care for them. Add making cookies for your neighbors as an item on your "to do" list for the year 2000.

FINAL THOUGHT

Remember: Good neighbors are chocolate chips in the cookies of life!

READ ALEXIS de TOCQUEVILLE'S
DEMOCRACY IN AMERICA

"When people start standing in line to get out of this country instead of standing in line to get in, then we can start worrying about our system."

—Anonymous

Tocqueville was born in 1805, shortly after the French Revolution. He was a man who loved the concept of democracy and fought for his people's rights and independence. At age twenty-five, Tocqueville came to America. He traveled many thousands of miles and was overwhelmed and intrigued by America. His fourteen notebooks of observations became the basis for *Democracy in America,* released in 1835.

Democracy in America is arguably one of the most penetrating analyses of American life and government ever written. Two views emerge from the book:

- Tocqueville was intensely disturbed by the welfare system. He spoke and fought strongly against the government's taking from the wealthy to subsidize the poor. He felt that the welfare system created idleness rather than inspiring and encouraging initiative.

- He was intrigued with the close union between religion and liberty. He saw how American society was benefiting from the influence of religion in daily life.

Tocqueville is probably best know
"America is great because America
ceases to be good, it will cease to be

There is no better time than the
America stood for 170 years ago an

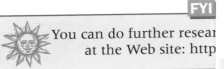

FYI

You can do further resear
at the Web site: http

CREATE A TIME CAPSULE FOR YOUR DESCENDANTS

"The only thing you take
with you when
you're gone
is what
you leave
behind."

—John Allston

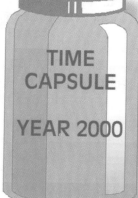

Time capsules, in some form, have been around since the appearance of humans. Some of the earliest time capsules were the Egyptian pyramids. These became repositories for the pharaohs as they prepared for a comfortable pilgrimage to the next world. During the 1964 World's Fair a time capsule was buried that was to be opened in 6964. Inside were such items as a newspaper, a bikini, and a Beatles record.

As you face a new millennium, what an opportunity you have to share with your descendants—your grandchildren, great-grandchildren, and even great-great-grandchildren—some of your family history, personal values, and religious heritage. Record your culture, values, and legacy, and save them in a time capsule.

Your time capsule could include:

- Photographs or a videotape of your family, your house, and your neighborhood.
- A newspaper from January 1, 2000.
- A bank passbook. Open a bank account, deposit ten dollars, and let your descendants discover its worth in 50 or 100 years.
- A list of the 100 most important things that have happened in your life.
- A written testimony of your personal faith.

FYI

Endless helps are available on the Internet.
Investigate the following Web site:
www.futurearchaeology.com.

101 Things To Do In The Year 2000

WRITE A LETTER TO THE EDITOR EXPRESSING YOUR VIEWS

"Public opinion is just a private opinion that makes enough noise to be heard."

—Anonymous

Do you read letters to the editor in newspapers and magazines? Some are brilliant and thought provoking; others are incoherent and pointless. But one thing stands out about these letters: No matter how exceptional, unsound, or offensive, some man or woman took the time to share an opinion. What may actually be said is not as important as simply taking the time to express one's feelings. There are few things that stir one's creative energy more than attempting to write a succinct statement of one's personal feelings, insights, concerns, and reactions.

Have you ever penned your own letter? Is there some topic in which you strongly believe or a controversy that riles you? Do you have strong opinions about prayer in school? How about school uniforms? Where do you stand on abortion? Do you approve of the way Congress spends your tax dollars? How about neighbors who let their dogs run wild? Or maybe you violently disagree with an individual who wrote a previously published letter to the editor. The topics are endless.

With the dawn of the new millennium, you have a wonderful opportunity to let yourself be heard. Determine to take a stand for what you believe to be right and honorable. Let your community know your convictions. You may be surprised by the response.

FYI

Letters should include full name, address, and telephone number. Required length of a letter varies by newspaper from 150 to 500 words. Letters are usually subject to editing for length, possibility of libel, and accuracy of content.

GET IN TOUCH WITH THE
SPIRITUAL SIDE OF YOUR LIFE

"God gives nothing to those who keep their arms crossed."

—West African proverb

In recent years many of the top-selling titles on the *New York Times Best-sellers List* have dealt with the spiritual side of life with titles such as *Conversations with God, Simple Abundance, Chicken Soup for the Soul,* and *Traveling Mercies.*

But why this renewed interest in spiritual matters? Is there something in an individual that knows or aspires for more than the physical? Could humans be more than just glorified, well-developed, living organisms? Two answers are possible:

Basic premise #1: A human being is a living organism, just like any plant or animal. Each of these organisms has a physical body—something one can see and touch. Each shows a level or degree of life that can be observed. It can be discerned when an organism is living and when it is dead.

Basic premise #2: A human being has a spiritual self that is not shared by plants and animals. Humans can think, reason, plan, and teach. In addition, humans appear to have a spiritual vacuum that yearns to be filled. This yearning is the basis for the current interest in spirituality.

The concluding assumption: If there is a spiritual side to existence, should we not begin exploring this aspect of our lives? Since we are more than plants or animals, it behooves us to begin investigating.

THE NEXT STEP

Why not plan for the year 2000 to be the time that you think seriously about who you are, where you came from, and where you are going?

TRACE YOUR FAMILY TREE

"I don't know who my grandfather was; I am much more concerned to know what his grandson will be."

—Abraham Lincoln

There is a natural curiosity about the past. This inquisitiveness extends beyond fun and games for the young. Almost everyone would like to know his or her family heritage. Consider tracing your family tree as one of your goals for the year 2000. It can become an absorbing and rewarding hobby. Who knows where it might lead? You might discover a relative who arrived on the Mayflower, a royal ancestor, or possibly a villain that you would just as soon forget. Even the best of family trees have some sap and will produce some nuts!

The point in doing this research and producing a family tree is that you'll be creating a valuable resource to share with your family as well as discovering fascinating insight into your own life. Where do you begin?

- To make the project relatively easy, you need a computer. This allows you to store names, dates, documents, and all other data.

- Next you need to purchase software to construct your family tree—such as the *Family Tree Maker*. This software producer also has a wonderful Web site at www.familytreemaker.com.

- Finally, make use of the Internet to check out other sites like www.genealogy.tbox.com and www.rootsweb.com.

FYI

An excellent resource book for family research on the Web is *Searching for Cyber-Root*, by Laurie and Steve Bonner.

101 Things To Do In The Year 2000

SPEND A SATURDAY AFTERNOON AT THE LIBRARY

"What we become depends on what we read after all of the professors have finished with us. The greatest university of all is a collection of books."

—Thomas Carlyle

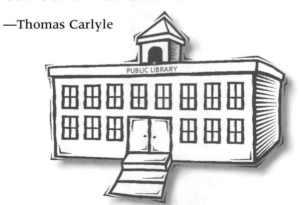

Your neighborhood library provides a vast array of resources, and its use is nearly always totally free. It can fulfill any of the following needs and wants.

- Want to read the latest best-selling novel?
- Interested in renting and watching an adventure video for a small fee?
- Do you like magazines? You will find dozens, even hundreds, of current magazines and daily newspapers available.
- Are you looking for an array of large-print books?
- Do you need additional information on a special project?
- Are you looking for books and audios for your children?
- Have you wanted to try the Internet but needed some help?
- Would you like to pick up copies of the latest federal income tax forms?
- Is there a book that you want but can't locate? Ask the library to order it from another on their interlibrary loan program.
- Are you looking for a fun, enriching, and relaxing atmosphere?

Spending a Saturday afternoon at your nearest library will amaze you with what it has to offer you and your family.

THE NEXT STEP

If you have not utilized the vast resources available at the public library, plan to make the year 2000 a time for investigation. Best of all, there's no admission charge!

PREPARE A JOURNAL OR DIARY DURING THE YEAR 2000

"You are today where your thoughts have brought you; you will be tomorrow where your thoughts take you."

—James Allen

One of the best-known dramatizations of all time is a film entitled *The Diary of Anne Frank*. It is based on the diary of a Jewish girl who spent two years hiding in an attic in Amsterdam, Netherlands, to avoid arrest by the Nazis and deportation to a concentration camp. Anne records in her diary how fearful and wearisome the ordeal is as she and her family hide in those close quarters. One frightened young girl's recorded account of her inner thoughts and observations has had an impact upon the lives of millions.

Fortunately, you have probably not experienced the terror of the Nazi regime. Yet, to think that you will be experiencing a new millennium—that you will actually be living in the year 2000—should be an incentive to jot down in a diary or journal some of the personal highlights of this year.

You will probably not impact thousands as Anne Frank did with her diary, but your diary can have a positive impact upon your life and the generations that follow in your family.

These entries should document information about your experiences, celebrations, highlights, and personal insights that happen during the year. Not only will it be enjoyable and illuminating to read in the years to come, but also it will be a valuable historical record.

FINAL THOUGHT

There are few things that your children and grand-children will treasure more than your own personal account of what happened in the year 2000.

101 Things To Do In The Year 2000

SHARE YOUR OPINIONS WITH YOUR REPRESENTATIVES AND SENATORS

"Science may have found a cure for most evils, but it has found no remedy for the worst of them all: the apathy of human beings."

—Helen Keller

The story is told of a professor who asked his class, "Who can define the term *apathy*?" Wherein one of the students responded, "I don't know and I don't care."

We don't see ourselves as apathetic about our government. True, there are 1001 things that we would like to see our public officials do differently, and there are even times when we openly share our political opinions with our friends. But normally these personal opinions are never communicated to our congressional leaders.

How would you define apathy? Isn't it to be indifferent and completely unconcerned—to be without feeling and have no interest?

If less than 50 percent of the populace vote in a national election and most shrug off voting by saying one single vote does not mean anything, isn't that apathy? And if 90 percent or more of the public never communicate their convictions to their representatives or senators, isn't that apathy?

To make a democratic government work, citizens have the responsibility to keep their senators and representatives up to speed on their opinions concerning specific issues.

As you enter into a new millennium, government issues will become even more complex. Therefore, it's extremely imperative in the year 2000 that you communicate with your elected officials.

Communicating is easier than ever with the Internet: http://unitedseniors.org/contact.html and www.2020vision.org/contact.html.

TRY ONE NEW RECIPE EVERY MONTH FOR A YEAR

"Cooking is like love. It should be entered into with abandon or not at all."

—Harriet Van Horne

19

Has macaroni and cheese become a once-a-week dish at your house? Are your kids begging you to "fix something different for dinner like Grandma does"? Families often get into a rut and eat only about ten basic meals.

During this special celebration year, why not venture out? Why not be adventuresome? Why not try one totally new recipe every month during the year? You don't need to be a great cook; you don't need to take cooking classes. You just need to be determined to find one new recipe that you will try during the month and then go to it. Make it a goal. Maybe a different member of the family will be responsible for finding the new recipe each month. Maybe you can make the recipe of the month the basis for an ethnic celebration. The new recipe could be anything from a great casserole to a sumptuous soup or a spectacular dessert.

Hints for finding new recipes:

- Newspapers feature dozens of new recipes and cooking ideas.
- Bookstores, as well as the public library, are loaded with cookbooks.
- Cookbooks are now on computer software with thousands of recipes.
- Ask a friend, parent, or relative for one of their favorite recipes.

Some wonderful resource magazines are *The Taste of Home* and *Taste of Home's Quick Cooking*. They can be contacted at 800-344-6913 or at www.reinmanpub.com.

WRITE A LETTER TO YOUR CHILDREN EXPRESSING YOUR LOVE

"Give a little love to a child, and you get a great deal back."

—John Ruskin

20

Dear Ben:

There are probably few words that you need to hear more than what I am going to say: I am proud of you. I am extremely happy that you are my son. And I love you very much.

It's true, there have been times when we have had our differences, but the negative times pale in comparison to the joy and cheer that you have brought to my life. When you were born, it was one of the great thrills of my life. As I look back and reflect on all our great times together, it brings tears to my eyes. I remember when . . .

Love, Dad

Family life is filled with both joys and frustrations. We need to consciously remind ourselves—and our children—that no matter how many ups and downs there have been, we have always loved and appreciated our children.

When was the last time you wrote a note or sent a card expressing your love to your offspring? When was the last time you actually said to your children, "I love you"? There are few things that you can do that will be more appreciated.

THE NEXT STEP

Make the year 2000 the year that you connect with your children and grandchildren and express those inner feelings of love outwardly.

SET A GOAL TO LOSE THE
WEIGHT YOU GAINED LAST YEAR

"O! that this too solid flesh
would melt."

—William Shakespeare

21

It's been said that Americans have more food to eat than any other people on earth . . . and more diets to keep them from eating it. Dieting has become almost as American as baseball and apple pie . . . well, maybe sugarless apple pie.

As the old year checks out and the new year rolls in, people invariably begin making resolutions to lose weight. Diet books clog the shelves in bookstores; pharmacies promote the latest diet fads; and sporting goods stores have all the exercise equipment on sale "at the lowest prices in history."

But statistics say that most dieters gain back what they lose—they are simply on yo-yo diets. As the years increase, so do the pounds. What can you do to keep off the weight you lose this year?

- First, you must resolve that you want to lose those extra pounds during the new year—no matter what the cost. You need to make some type of binding promise.
- Next, set a simple, realistic, and attainable goal—maybe to lose all the weight that you gained last year.
- Finally, break your goal down into reasonable portions. If you gained ten pounds, you will need to lose less than one pound per month. Your goal: Lose one pound per month.

It can be easy if you set a goal and resolve with every fiber of your being to keep your resolution. That's the secret.

FYI

The Resolution Diet by David Heber might provide added assistance.

SIGN UP FOR A
DALE CARNEGIE COURSE

"All of us do not have equal talent, but all of us should have an equal opportunity to develop our talent."

—John F. Kennedy

22

Dale Carnegie's personality is embedded in the nationwide courses that bear his name. Going beyond merely teaching public speaking skills, Carnegie discovered the chicken-and-egg connection between speaking well and having a positive self-perception.

Responses from people who have taken the Dale Carnegie Course are hard to believe. Participants give it praise for making them better employees, motivating them to higher achievement, and helping them become better parents.

What is it about the Dale Carnegie Course that inspires such enthusiasm?

Here is a list of rewards to be gained from the Dale Carnegie Course:

- Confidence to overcome society's number one fear— speaking in front of people.
- Enhanced communication skills.
- Valuable principles of memorization.
- Principles and skills for strong leadership.
- Methods for improving relationships.
- Lessons in how to sell yourself and your ideas.
- Insights into motivation, morale, and teamwork.

THE NEXT STEP

As you kick off a new millennium, give consideration to what the world-famous Dale Carnegie Course can do for you, your family, and your job. Check it out. It's a great investment for the year 2000 and beyond.

VISIT YOUR STATE CAPITOL AND OTHER STATE LANDMARKS

"What's the difference between the American dream and everyone else's dream? Everyone else's dream is to come to America."

—Anonymous

23

Most of us feel that vacation means doing something special with our family, something out of the ordinary that calls for a trip far from home. If we live in Virginia, vacation means going to Yellowstone Park. If we live in Michigan, vacation means going to San Francisco.

But such vacation planning may stretch the budget to the breaking point and lead to some hard choices—not to mention wear and tear on family relationships. Two thousand miles together in a car can seem like three, especially with children.

Before you plan such a trip with your family, get to know your own state first. Have you visited your state Capitol? The homes of your state founders? Your state library? Your governor's residence? Have you seen your state legislature in session? Most states have maps showing a list of historical markers throughout the state. A tour of such markers makes an entertaining and educational trip. Plan in the year 2000 to spend time investigating the landmarks and fun spots in your own state.

Many historical sites have been set aside as state parks with hotel accommodations as well as campsites for overnight lodging. There are often recreational developments nearby.

FYI

A good place to start gathering information is your state's office of tourism.

101 Things To Do In The Year **2000**

SURPRISE YOUR SPOUSE WITH A CANDLELIGHT DINNER

"To love and be loved is to feel the sun from both sides."

—David Viscott

24

Work situations seem to be more and more demanding for both men and women as we cross the threshold to a new millennium. The old pattern of working five days a week and having two off for home, family, church, and other interests has given way to twelve-hour days nonstop for two weeks, business travel over weekends to save expenses on airfare, and cell phones and pagers to keep us at the beck and call of our employers.

It's easier than ever to forget the little things that often say the most to a husband or wife. Resolve now to redeem the situation with a surprise candlelight dinner in the year 2000.

Your secret planning could include:

- Deciding on a menu with at least one of your spouse's favorite dishes.
- Preparing the food or ordering it from a takeout service.
- Stopping at a card store for that special message and perhaps a favor.
- Picking up flowers from a florist or a street vendor.
- Arranging for childcare so the two of you can be alone.

And don't forget the candles! You will have a ball preparing and decorating and keeping it all a secret. Part of the fun is anticipating the surprise on your loved one's face. He or she may respond with open-mouthed astonishment or with tears.

FINAL THOUGHT

A surprise candlelight dinner yells loud and clear
—I love you!

101 Things To Do In The Year **2000**

RENT THE VIDEO *SHADOWLANDS* **AND WATCH IT WITH YOUR SPOUSE**

"Faith assures us of things we expect and convinces us of the existence of things we cannot see."

—Hebrews 11:1, GOD'S WORD

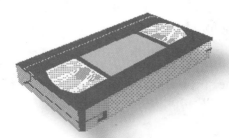

25

Few movies have touched me like *Shadowlands*. It was one of the most honest, romantic, meaningful, and inspiring movies I've ever seen.

Shadowlands is the fictionalized depiction of the romance between scholar and author C. S. Lewis (1898-1963) and American poet Joy Gresham. It is set against the majesty of Oxford University and in the shadow of a nearby hospital room. In the movie, Anthony Hopkins and Debra Winger play the parts of Lewis and Gresham.

C. S. "Jack" Lewis was a classicist professor, Anglican theologian, and author. In the movie, he lives a canned life—he knows the answers to all the questions. In the classes he teaches, he is assured and brilliant. Over the course of seven years, his correspondence with Joy Gresham leads to friendship, love, and marriage, only to have their bond cut short by her death from cancer.

Suddenly Lewis comes face to face with questions he can't answer. He is uncertain about how God deals with humanity. One memorable scene depicts Lewis railing against God, who he believes has given happiness and then taken it away. Lewis struggles with his grief and finds a reason for living in becoming responsible for Joy Gresham's young son.

Suggestion for an evening in the year 2000: Make reservations at a nice restaurant and enjoy dinner with your husband or wife. Conclude the evening by going home and watching the video *Shadowlands*.

FINAL THOUGHT

Rejoice that you can experience the dawning of a new millennium together.

ORGANIZE YOUR
HOME FILING SYSTEM

"The beginning is the most important part of the work."

—Plato

26

John Devereaux felt he had lost his battle with clutter. There was a towering fortress of books, file folders, mail, brochures, and articles from the newspaper—not to mention every golf magazine known to humankind for the last ten years. John's philosophy was, "Pile it now and file it later." Do you have any suggestions for John?

More than anything else, John needs determination to make a change. Second, he needs a strategy for precisely what he wants to accomplish in setting up a filing system. Next, he desperately needs advice as to how to categorize his files. Finally, he needs a garbage can!

Some helpful tips for John and for you:

- Files should be within reach as John sits in his office chair. He might consider purchasing a file with wheels. If he has to get up and move, he very likely will pile rather than file.

- John needs to set aside at least a half-day, or even a full day, to complete this task.

- John needs to know that the 80/20 rule still applies—he will only refer to about 20 percent of the things he has saved.

- Finally, a good filing system is not for storage but for retrieval.

Many people face the dilemma of organizing a filing system. Make the year 2000 the year that you organize your home filing system.

FYI

You will find excellent suggestions in the book
Organizing from the Inside Out
by Julie Morgenstern.

HAVE A FAMILY PHOTOGRAPH TAKEN

"Gratitude is the fairest blossom which springs from the soul."

—Henry Ward Beecher

27

Shopping for gifts, particularly gifts for parents and family members, can be a nightmare. What can you give your mother who already seems to have everything? Perhaps your dad is the one who is hard to please, or your brother who always exchanges everything you pick out for him.

Your friends and family have no doubt had that same problem when shopping for you. Without a doubt, there have been times when you've received the latest gadget or newest widget as a present during the holiday season or for a birthday. You may have even used it once or twice, but probably it's in a drawer, forgotten.

If you're looking for a gift that will be deeply appreciated and will keep on giving, consider having a family portrait made. Not only is it a thoughtful choice for now, but it will be appreciated by family and friends for years to come. It also simplifies shopping since you can give the photograph to almost everyone on your list.

Portrait considerations before you go include: the background scenery— whether indoor or outdoor; type and color of clothing —consider fun motifs like western outfits or ski clothes; date of photograph—could be anniversary, graduation, or to include a new baby.

THE NEXT STEP

There's no more appropriate time for a family portrait than the beginning of a new millennial year. The recipients of your portrait will be grateful for such a gift, and so will you.

101 Things To Do In The Year **2000**

VISIT A MUSEUM,
AN AQUARIUM, OR A ZOO

"True enjoyment comes
from activity of the mind
and exercise of the body;
the two are ever united."

—Wilhelm von Humboldt

28

Of all the memories from my childhood, nothing compares to the school trips to Chicago to visit the Museum of Science and Industry, the Natural History Museum, the Shedd Aquarium, and the Brookfield Zoo. These marvelous adventures are still indelibly impressed upon my mind.

As the new millennium dawns, plan a day or a weekend trip to a local museum, aquarium, or zoo. If you have children or grandchildren, this is a wonderful learning adventure for everyone involved, as well as a time for further bonding. Memories of these experiences will last a lifetime. This is a marvelous manner in which to celebrate the year 2000.

- If you are interested in visiting an aquarium, the following Web site is filled with information and links to nationwide aquariums: http://www.scubaonline.com/aqua.html.

- For information on over 900 museums worldwide, check out the following Web site, which is filled with unbelievable information: http://wwar.com/museums.html.

- If you are enticed by a zoo, be sure to gather some incredible information from this Web site: http://www.zooweb.net.

Outstanding travel and tour books, complete with information on zoos, aquariums, and museums, can be found in the library and your local bookstore.

101 Things To Do In The Year **2000**

BUY A CLEAN JOKE BOOK AND MEMORIZE A HANDFUL FOR TELLING ON ANY OCCASION

"Those who bring sunshine to the lives of others cannot keep it from themselves."

—James Matthew Barrie

29

As the flood subsided, Noah opened the doors of the Ark and released the animals. All living things rushed to freedom, except for two snakes that lingered in a corner. "Why don't you go forth and multiply?" asked Noah in a stern voice. "We can't," moaned one. "We're adders!"

How many times have you thought to yourself: I wish I could remember some of the good clean jokes I've heard. I forget them almost immediately. I'd give anything if I could remember one of those stories.

Almost every day, people hear a new joke. The big problem is that the majority of the stories told on the job are off-color. If you're like most people, you would love to remember and retell the jokes you hear, at least the ones that don't have a risqué slant. Jokes invigorate and regenerate with their laughter, and they can turn a sour situation into a positive one.

Our suggestion: Buy a humor book filled with good clean jokes. Read it, find a handful of jokes that strike your funny bone, and then memorize them. Then at the next meeting around the water cooler or at lunch, become the life of the gathering with some good clean fun. Put this on your "to do" list as you prepare for the year 2000.

Two great resources for good, clean fun and laughs: *An Encyclopedia of Humor* by Lowell Streiker and the Internet site www.gcfl.com.

ERECT A BIRD FEEDER AND BIRDBATH

"I value my garden more for being full of blackbirds than of cherries, and very frankly give them fruit for their songs."

—Joseph Addison

30

My mother and father had a popular, outdoor pastime—feeding and watching birds. Or was it an indoor pastime? Either way, the satisfaction of attracting birds brought immense joy to both of them. Even after my father became debilitated by Parkinson's disease, he would sit by the window with his binoculars and bird book and endlessly watch the comings and goings of all types of birds. Few things brought him greater joy. My mother still keeps numerous bird feeders filled with feed, both summer and winter. Her cluster of bird feeders includes an open feeder, a platform feeder, a tube feeder, and a hummingbird feeder, plus a beautiful birdbath. Today my mother's backyard is filled with cardinals, finches, robins, orioles, grosbeaks, blue jays, and hummingbirds.

For my parents, attracting and watching birds became an addiction. They would call long-distance just to tell me about the newest birds they had seen. If you've never experienced the thrill of watching and feeding birds, why not begin the new millennium by caring for some of God's little creatures?

To attract birds to a site, feed them during all four seasons, placing the feeders in clusters of twos and threes.

To attract birds to a birdbath, place it in the open where the birds flying overhead can spot it. Locate it in a sunny spot, but situate it close to trees where the birds can perch to dry off.

 For books on building birdhouses and birdbaths contact: http://amazon.com and http://barnesandnoble.com.

FORGIVE ANY LONGSTANDING GRUDGE

"To err is human, to forgive divine."

—Alexander Pope

31

Why do the British drive on the left side of the road? H. Allen Smith offers this explanation: The Pope came to Paris and until then there was no rule governing the movement of "horse" traffic. It was decreed that during the Pope's visit Parisians should ride on the right side, leaving the left side clear for the Pope. Napoleon later made it the law of the land. The British so hated Napoleon that they reversed the custom.

The British definitely had a grudge against the French, and probably the French against the British at that point in history.

A grudge is like a dandelion with an unseen, hidden root. You can cut off the flower and the greens, and even try to dig out the root, but you don't always eradicate the dandelion. The root goes much deeper than imagined. And in a short time the dandelion is blooming again.

A grudge has a deeper root than most people assume. That strong, continued feeling of bitterness and resentment over a real or imaginary grievance can sink deep into one's soul.

To experience life on the highest level, you must eliminate any longstanding grudges—completely. Often this calls for communicating openly with the person by whom you were offended. When the situation is known and resolved by both parties, you will be on your way to healing.

FINAL THOUGHT

Don't allow a bitter root of resentment to grow within you. Make a firm resolution that in the year 2000 you are going to forgive anyone and everyone who has wronged you, be the situation real or imaginary.

SAVE 5 PERCENT OF
EACH PAYCHECK AND INVEST IT

"Annual income
twenty pounds, annual
expenditure nineteen
six, result
happiness.
Annual income
twenty pounds,
annual
expenditure
twenty pounds
ought six, result misery."

—Charles Dickens

32

According to recent studies, the following is true:

- About four out of 10 U.S. households have no retirement savings at all.
- Today's average fifty-year-old has only about $2,300 in savings.
- About 40 percent of the people ages fifty-one to sixty-one expect to have no retirement income except social security.

Frightening, isn't it? How about you? How are you doing with your savings plans? Like a golfer following a set routine in lining up a putt, individuals need a set routine for saving money—and the discipline to practice it.

When it comes to saving, almost everyone procrastinates. Probably the best way to begin to save is to set up some type of automatic savings withdrawal plan. The assumption is that if you don't see it and don't handle it—you won't spend it. By using an automatic withdrawal plan, you're paying yourself before you pay creditors.

Save 5 percent of everything you make. If your check is for $1000 per week, have $50 deducted and automatically placed into a savings program, a company 401(k) program, or a mutual fund. As the savings nest egg increases and your confidence grows, you can increase the percentage.

THE NEXT STEP

Make "pay yourself first" your new rule as you enter into the year 2000.

EAT A PINT OF GOURMET ICE CREAM

"I doubt whether the world holds for anyone a more soul-stirring surprise than the first adventure with ice cream."

—Heywood Broun

33

Legends swirl around the origins of ice cream. Some think it originated in China around 2000 B.C. Others tell us that Alexander the Great and the emperor Nero ate snow flavored with honey and fruit. Marco Polo is said to have tasted ice cream on his thirteenth-century visit to China and then introduced a frozen dessert when he returned to Italy. In the seventeenth century, Italy introduced gelati, a flavored ice made with cream.

Ice cream was first mentioned in the early colonies in the 1700s. Reportedly, George Washington spent $200 on ice cream in New York in the summer of 1790. Thomas Jefferson and Dolly Madison were early connoisseurs of ice cream. It was served at the second inaugural ball in 1812. In 1851 a Baltimore dairyman, Jacob Fussell, began the commercial production of ice cream. And as they say, the rest is history.

Today, according to the International Ice Cream Association, the United States produces more than 1.5 billion gallons of ice cream and frozen desserts annually.

You've probably had your favorite flavor of gourmet ice cream beckon to you on more than one occasion from the frozen food section of your grocery store.

THE NEXT STEP

Celebrate the year 2000 and indulge yourself for once. Buy a pint and eat every last bit of it by yourself. You deserve it!

TURN OFF THE TV FOR A DAY OR A WEEK

"All television is educational television. The question is what is it teaching?"

—Nicholas Johnson

34

In Russia's St. Petersburg Zoo, the zookeepers placed a television outside the cage of a pair of orangutans. The reasoning was that if the primates saw numerous videos on adult parenting skills, they might adopt them. However, Rabu, the male orangutan, became so engrossed in the videos that he started to neglect his mate and their offspring.

This story would be funny if it weren't so sad. It's a frightening indictment of the effects of television watching upon a family. Instead of drawing the household together, TV has the after-effect of fracturing the family. In one sense, television has turned the family circle into a half circle. Communication has vanished as the family stares for hours on end at the TV set.

Beyond potentially severing the family, researchers tell us that television affects a child's concept of right and wrong. Statistics affirm that the average child, by the age of eighteen, will have viewed 25,000 murders and countless thousands of adulterous situations. It has been said that while the Roman Empire was crumbling, the people remained reasonably happy with the circuses. Today it's television.

FINAL THOUGHT

Why not take the Y2K challenge? Turn off your TV for a day or even a week. Forget about your favorite TV shows. Focus on your family and their needs. Spend time getting to know one another again. The world would be better off with less television and more vision.

CARRY A $100 BILL WITH YOU AT ALL TIMES

> "The safest way to double
> your money is to fold it
> over once and put it in your
> pocket."
>
> —Kin Hubbard

35

In a society that uses less cash by the day, where everyone has credit cards, and where ATMs are as prevalent as fast-food restaurants, why should you carry any cash at all, let alone a $100 bill? There are a number of good reasons:

- It's always there for emergencies (which could turn out to be more than just embarrassing).

- It provides a certain amount of security—like having a financial bodyguard.

- It has the tendency to elevate one's self-esteem.

- Amazingly, there are still places that don't take credit cards. Maybe you have been in a situation where your credit card would not ring through for verification or for some reason it was put on hold. What a relief to have that extra $100 tucked away.

- One bill can be folded up and hidden away in your billfold or purse. Don't fold up five $20 bills, but secure one $100 bill, for the psychological boost as well as the safety.

- Don't tell anyone what you have done. This is your own little secret, but I do guarantee you that it will have a positive effect on your life.

FINAL THOUGHT

Wow! What a way to start out the year 2000—with $100 hidden away in your billfold or purse, always there and always ready.

101 Things To Do In The Year 2000

JOIN A BOOK CLUB OR BOOK DISCUSSION GROUP

"I cannot live without books."

—Thomas Jefferson

36

If you read magazines, you have seen advertisements to join a book club. Most book clubs offer great deals and are well worth investigating. Conceivably, you could acquire up to $125 worth of books for about $1 plus $14 in shipping. During the next two years, you may only have to spend $50 plus shipping to meet your club's obligations.

Book clubs are available to meet almost any interest: recent releases, religion, cooking, business and management, mystery, gardening, parenting, children's interests, and many others. Being part of a book club is a fun experience. Not only do you receive books at a good price, but you also receive monthly updates on the newest books to hit the market.

Once you have bought and received your selection, you may want to discuss it with others. Search out a book discussion group in your area. Such groups usually meet once a month with an assigned title for reading and discussion. This type of group normally comprises what I call *bookaholics*—they love just being around books and they love discussing them. It's an enlightening and refreshing experience that will stretch your mind as you share your perceptions of various themes found in the selected book.

THE NEXT STEP

 Determine now to join a book club or book discussion group during the year 2000, and then have a ball reading and discussing your new books with new friends.

LEARN TO ROLLERBLADE

"Heroes are not the ones
that never fail, but the ones
who never give up."

—Ed Cole

37

One of the fastest growing sports in America today is Rollerblading (also known as in-line skating). Rollerbladers run the gamut from four-year-olds to eighty-four-year-olds. There is almost no age barrier for this sport. Yearly sales of Rollerblades are an estimated twenty million units. For those unfamiliar with this sport, a Rollerblade or in-line skate is a lightweight, hard plastic boot with three to five wheels fastened in a line under the sole of the boot.

If you've ever felt a need to get more exercise but get bored with aerobics, treadmills, and weight lifting, why not try Rollerblading? It's a fun alternative to jogging, yet it will give you a thorough workout. Rollerblading will have you huffing and puffing and asking for more. The end result: You will feel better about yourself and about life.

On an average, a pair of in-line skates weighs between four and seven pounds. Adult skates will run as low at $40, but the better skates will cost between $100 and $200 and can run as high as $500. Some centers allow you to rent them. If classes are available and you feel unsure as you start, you might consider taking a class or two. Because the hardest thing about in-line skating is the cement or hard surface on which you skate, you will also want to consider wearing protective gear—elbow, wrist, and knee guards as well as a helmet.

THE NEXT STEP

Be adventuresome. Why not give Rollerblading a spin during the new year?

VOLUNTEER FOR A COMMUNITY PROJECT

"My grandfather once told me that there were two kinds of people: those who do the work and those who take the credit. He told me to try to be in the first group; there was much less competition."

—Indira Ghandi

38

Habitat for Humanity International builds or rehabilitates homes for families that are in need. To date over 70,000 homes and 350,000 people around the world have received affordable, decent housing as a result of Habitat efforts. These houses are built and sold to the partner families at no profit to the builders and with no-interest loans. The monthly mortgage payments are recycled back into the Habitat fund to build more houses.

Currently there are over 1,400 affiliates in the United States and 300 more international affiliates. As you can well imagine, volunteers are one of the big needs. People who get involved do so out of concern and love for others. Numerous churches and college student groups are actively involved. The most famous volunteers, of course, are former President Jimmy Carter and his wife, Rosalyn Carter. "It's a wonderful experience for us," they declare.

As the new millennial year dawns, make positive plans to give a week or more as a volunteer for Habitat for Humanity. Not only will you be helping provide a home for a family that could not have one otherwise, you will be part of a group effort that is well organized and efficient. "Every drop of sweat is worth it," say Betty and Seff Polk who worked with Habitat for Humanity to build their own house.

FYI

 Habitat for Humanity can be contacted at 912-924-6935 or on the Internet at www.habitat.org.

TREAT A COWORKER TO LUNCH

"How about getting together for lunch next week? My treat."

—overheard at the water cooler

39

Business leaders suggest that there's value in inviting your coworkers to lunch from time to time. The lunchtime colleagues don't have to be only from your department; invite personnel from other departments or divisions. This is particularly true when your work intersects with theirs.

Taking a coworker to lunch provides a number of personal benefits.

- Getting to know them, their family, and their early backgrounds.

- Learning how your jobs intersect—where they're similar and how they differ.

- Discovering similarities in hobbies and interests. Knowing a person is a gardener or a golfer can often translate into passing along spring bulbs or a sleeve of golf balls.

- Acquiring the date of their birthday for future greeting card reference.

- There may even be times when you need their support or assistance on a project—perhaps something as small as getting a check cut. With your developing relationship, you will feel freer to ask.

THE NEXT STEP

As you focus on the new millennial year at work, make definite plans to "spring" for lunch for one or more of your coworkers. Not only is it a good business move, but you might make a new friend at the same time.

101 Things To Do In The Year **2000**

LEARN A FOREIGN LANGUAGE

"The three-legged stool of understanding is held up by history, languages, and mathematics. Equipped with these three you can learn anything you want to learn. But if you lack any one of them you are just another ignorant peasant."

—Robert Heinlein

40

The Bible says that our ancient ancestors spoke only one language and had a common speech. This was true for many, many generations. Communication was easy; foreign languages were unknown, even in Noah's time. But rebelliousness and pride, as well as a desire to build a tower to heaven, reared their ugly heads. As a result, the Bible reports, God punished humankind by confusing this universal, common language and it became "babble." From this series of events is derived the story of the Tower of Babel.

Forty-five hundred years later many people still look at learning a new language as a punishment when in reality it is an exciting challenge. Everyone has the ability to learn a foreign language. Look at a young child whose beginning language is babble but who easily learns his or her mother tongue. If a baby can learn a new language, why can't you? There are great positive benefits in learning a second language.

- It increases job opportunities. The bilingual person has an advantage over the person who speaks only one language.
- It enhances travel and vacation time. If you plan to vacation in Mexico, learning Spanish will add to your enjoyment.
- It will have a positive effect on your intellectual growth.
- It opens doors of interest to other cultures.

FYI

Web site for foreign language information:
http://www.call.gov/index/htm.

101 Things To Do In The Year **2000**

WRITE A BRIEF ABOUT THE LAST YEAR OF YOUR LIFE

"If my doctor told me I only had six minutes to live, I wouldn't brood. I'd type a little faster."

—Isaac Asimov

41

Most people have the feeling that they are invincible. They have a hard time conceiving of life going on without them. To ponder and imagine that they might be the focal point of a funeral is not a pleasant thought. Most of us would rather think about almost anything else.

Let's suppose through some mysterious means that you discovered your life would end on January 1, 2001. How would you spend the last year of your life? Frightening question isn't it?

Here are some points to consider:

- Currently, your job probably plays a key, central role in your life. As you ruminate on the last year of your life, do you now wish you had spent more time at the office? Or do you wish that you had placed your family at the top of your list?

- Speaking of family, how much of the last year would you dedicate to your immediate family?

- How about your friends? Do you wish you had taken more time to make close friends? How would you allocate your time in the last year for your current friends?

- Would spiritual things be more important now? How would your relationship with God change as you witnessed your life coming to an end?

FINAL THOUGHT

Think through these questions. Summarize on paper some of the specific things that you would like to do during the last year of your life. Then make these items your focus for the year 2000.

101 Things To Do In The Year 2000

DISCOVER THE TRUE MEANING OF CHRISTMAS AND EASTER

"Jesus is the reason for the season."

42

It's your birthday, your special day! Family and friends have organized a thoughtful, joyous celebration. They know what you like and have made special preparations just for you—your favorite foods, your favorite everything. You feel honored, appreciated, and special. They love you and it shows.

Next year the party grows bigger and some folks become loud and obnoxious. But the personal attention is there and you're glad that at least they remembered your birthday. Most of the people in attendance you've never met. People no longer celebrate your birthday; for them it's "party time," and nobody greets you or even says "happy birthday." What has become of your special birthday celebration?

Christmas, in a sense, is a birthday celebration, but have Santa, Christmas trees, and presents become the focal point while the birthday observance is forgotten?

Granted, Christmas and Easter are religious holidays of more recent origin. But to have the focus of Christmas on Santa and presents and the focus of Easter on the Easter bunny and new spring fashions degenerates the original intent of the birth and resurrection of Jesus. Can there be a real Christmas and Easter without Jesus?

FINAL THOUGHT

 As you begin this wonderful new millennium, take a second look at the original intent and purpose of Christmas and Easter . . . and discover their true meanings.

PLANT A VEGETABLE GARDEN
AND SHARE THE PRODUCE

"Working in the garden . . .
gives me a profound feeling
of inner peace."

—Ruth Stout

There is nothing, as any gardener will tell you, more delicious than a big, red, juicy tomato straight off the vine, unless it's new sugary peas that have just been shelled, or the first picking of sweet corn, new potatoes, beets, radishes, onions, and lettuce.

In a space as small as seventy-five square feet, you can plant a phenomenal garden. If space is at a premium, you should consider buying some flowerpots that also can be used as decorative borders filled with tomatoes, onions, and herbs.

What's the advantage of raising vegetables? Why not just buy them at the store?

- The run-of-the-mill vegetables offered by local food chains and markets can't compare in taste and nutrition to fresh garden vegetables.
- Store-bought vegetables are normally laden with chemicals—artificial fertilizers, pesticides, and weed killers. These can be controlled in a home garden.
- You will find sheer delight in watching your plants grow and feeling the thrill of picking fresh, homegrown vegetables.
- The most excellent reason of all—it gives you the opportunity to share some of the labor of your love with your friends and neighbors.

THE NEXT STEP

 If you have never planted a vegetable garden, raise your own vegetables in the year 2000 to eat and to share.

LEARN ONE NEW WORD EVERY DAY

"The difference between the right word and the almost right word is the difference between lightning and the lightning bug."

—Mark Twain

44

When I walked into Richard's office, he was sitting at his desk with a tiny dictionary in his hands. I asked him what he was doing with the dictionary, and he said, "I've got this inner desire to expand my vocabulary." He explained that his job responsibility was pushing him to communicate with some new customers and he felt inadequate with his current vocabulary. As a positive move he was making it his responsibility to learn one new word daily.

Think about it—it's not hard to learn a new word each day, but it does take focus and commitment. Currently, there are approximately 300,000 English words recorded in the *Oxford English Dictionary* (thirteen volumes). Some scholars have estimated that there are close to 1,000,000 words in the English language when slang, scientific, and technical terms are included. Yet, it's estimated that the average college graduate has a vocabulary of only 30,000 words.

Set yourself a big goal for the year 2000—to learn one new word every day throughout the year. Increasing your vocabulary by 365 new words in one year is a phenomenal accomplishment. But if you were to learn one new word every day for twenty-five years, that increase of 9000 new words would place you among the elite in the world when it comes to vocabulary. This small commitment could pay a lifetime of dividends. Do you think you can do it?

Some great resources for building a bigger vocabulary are *Word-A-Day* calendars, *Word Builder* AudioTapes, and *Word-a-Day Vocabulary Builder* by Bergen Evans.

ASSEMBLE A LIST OF YOUR
STRENGTHS AND WEAKNESSES

"Every man is entitled to be valued by his best moment."

—Ralph Waldo Emerson

45

A common question for employers to ask in job interviews is, "Tell me about some of your strengths and some of your weaknesses." No matter how common, it usually hits a nerve with the prospective employee.

If you've never assessed your overall strengths and underlying weaknesses, that's a task that needs to be done during the year 2000. Not only will it aid you in future job interviews, but more important, it will enhance your self-worth. You need a current assessment of who you are—what you can do well and what you can't.

In your mind, go back to your school days and move forward in time. Jot down those circumstances that brought personal satisfaction as well as praise from others. At the same time, record some of the situations that were negative and brought some degree of censure.

Next take a piece of paper and draw a line down the middle. At the top of one side write *strengths* and at the top of the other side write *weaknesses*. Begin compiling your list. You may want to take a week or more to amass this list. Discuss the project and list with a friend or your spouse for input. Compile the list as one of your goals for the new millennium.

THE NEXT STEP

 As a result of this self-assessment, talk to your job supervisor or the director of human resources about your strengths. Consider taking some evening college classes. Use the strengths that you have noted as the foundation for a new and improved life.

MAKE THE PLATINUM RULE YOUR PERSONAL WORK PHILOSOPHY

> "Do unto others as they would like done unto them."
>
> — Tony Alessandra and Michael J. O'Connor in *The Platinum Rule*

46

The Golden Rule, as you know, says to treat others the way you want to be treated. This is an important axiom of life, but some business people have restated it and now call it the Platinum Rule.

Basically, the rule proposes that you help your coworkers, your employees, and your clients get what they want based on what is really important to them rather than how you, yourself, want to be treated.

Personalities are different. No two people are exactly the same. Each person has his or her own habits, idiosyncrasies, and ways of looking at the world. Hippocrates outlined four basic temperaments. If his assessment is correct, then probably three out of every four people have little desire to be treated as you crave to be treated.

What does all of this mean? It means that you must make it your responsibility to understand other people and treat them in a way that's best for them, not for you. It means taking the time to figure them out.

THE NEXT STEP

During the year 2000, read this enlightening book, *The Platinum Rule*, by Tony Alessandra and Michael J. O'Connor. Then put it into practice as you deal with people.

101 Things To Do In The Year 2000

FIND WAYS TO SIMPLIFY YOUR LIFE

"Our life is frittered away by detail. Simplicity, simplicity, simplicity!"

—Henry David Thoreau

47

Has your life become too complicated and cluttered by consumerism? Are you overstretched and overstressed? Do the demands on your life seem unbearable—both at home and at work?

Help comes for all of us in a superb resource book, *Simplify Your Life: 100 Ways to Slow Down and Enjoy the Things that Really Matter*, by Elaine St. James. This book is about gaining control of your life— in effect, creating more time to do the things that really matter to you.

There's no one "simplify your life" checklist that guarantees you're on the road to a simple lifestyle, but there are certain characteristics that permeate a simplified life. Hopefully, this list will point you in the right direction and furnish some impetus for simplifying your life.

- The simple life makes the workplace less important and your family more important.
- The simple life results in shopping less frequently for things that aren't needed as you attempt to escape the burden of debt.
- The simple life implies eating less quantity and eating less expensively.
- The simple life means simplifying your wardrobe, your bill-paying, and ultimately your whole approach to life.

FYI

Read the exceptional information available at this Web site: www.simpleliving.com.

PAY OFF ONE CREDIT CARD DURING THE YEAR

"Some debts are fun when you are acquiring them, but none are fun when you set about retiring them."

—Ogden Nash

48

Did you realize that if you have a $2,000 debt on a credit card at 21 percent interest and you pay only 2 percent of your balance every month, it will take you up to thirty years to pay off that debt? Scary, isn't it?

Financial planners tell us that when a person's credit card debt hits 20 percent of his or her gross income, that individual is probably in deep trouble.

If you find yourself making payments on two, three, or even more credit cards, make it your goal in the year 2000 to pay off at least one of these credit cards—even if it hurts. Determine the maximum dollars that you can pay monthly toward one specific card and make that your unswerving goal.

- Pay down your highest-interest credit card first.
- Search out the card with the lowest annual interest rate and consider moving the rest of your credit card debt into that debt account.
- Set up a stringent budget and follow it regularly. Investigate *Quicken* or *Microsoft Money* computer software. These top-of-the-line software partners will save you money and heartache.
- Never pay just the minimum payment on a credit card. If at all possible, pay off your credit cards monthly.

FYI

Good site for financial resources: http://www.pathfinder.com/money/plus/index.oft.

SET YOUR SIGHTS
ON WRITING YOUR FIRST BOOK

"The best time to plan a
book is while you're doing
the dishes."

—Agatha Christie

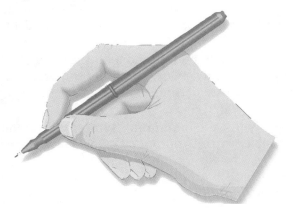

49

Who hasn't fantasized about writing a book—quitting the daily grind of eight-to-five and sitting all day at a computer developing intricate, mysterious plots or mind-boggling plans to change the world?

Of all the things that you could do in the year 2000, deciding to write a book may stretch you more than any other idea suggested in this book.

A few suggestions:

- Sign up for a writing course.
- Focus the topics of your writing in those areas you know the most about and have the deepest passion for.
- Set a goal to write a certain number of pages each week.
- Develop a first-rate book proposal that's really a sales presentation. Communicate why the book is important and salable.
- If a publisher shows interest, provide a top-quality presentation kit. Include a biographical sketch, a table of contents, a detailed outline, and three sample chapters.
- Stay away from "vanity" publishers who require you to pay before publishing your book.

FINAL THOUGHT

Don't plan to get rich by writing. The average book only sells about 5,000 copies and the royalties run less than a dollar per book. Do it for the joy, satisfaction, and discipline that are the end result.

101 Things To Do In The Year 2000

LEARN A NEW HOBBY THAT WILL ENHANCE YOUR LIFE

"Just don't give up trying to do what you really want to do. Where there is love and inspiration, I don't think you can go wrong."

—Ella Fitzgerald

50

Question: Who do you hear saying, "I'm bored to death"?

Answer: Young children, teenagers, housewives, singles, business people, assembly line workers, office workers, laborers, retirees, and on and on. Almost everyone at some time has made this statement.

Much of our nation's crime, lack of productivity on the job, marriage breakups, and even suicide can be traced to boredom.

Alan Caruba of the Boring Institute offers three suggestions that ensure that boredom will not be a factor in your life:

- Reading. The human mind demands stimulation of new knowledge, information, and insight.
- Hobbies. Everyone needs a hobby—some activity in which one can invest his or her passion.
- Be a joiner. Get out of the house. Join a group. Join several groups. Get involved in some organization. Get active!

Being a reader and a joiner are extremely important, but having a hobby may be the most important. Is there some leisure-time activity that you can throw yourself into recklessly and wholeheartedly? Make the decision now that during the year 2000 you will search out a new hobby. This resolution will greatly enrich your life. There are thousands of possibilities, from calligraphy to collecting antiques, from painting to photography.

A wonderful resource on the Internet for a variety of hobby and craft information is
http://azlist.miningco.com/index.htm.

BUY AN ELECTRONIC DARTBOARD AND DECLARE A TOURNAMENT

"Forget your opponents; always play against par."

—Sam Snead

51

There is something about playing darts that can really grow on you. The more you throw a dart at a target, the more you want to do it again and again—that bull's-eye seems so elusive.

Throwing darts is somewhat like golf or bowling, but probably more like archery. Each of these activities can be played against yourself or with partners in a competitive team setting. One truism about these sports is you always have that inner gnawing: "I know I can do better the next time. I just need to practice. I must concentrate and focus harder." There is always that "might have been" in competitive sports.

The game of darts has been and still is a popular game in England. The Pilgrims introduced it to America. With the arrival of computer chips, darts have undergone some radical changes. Instead of weighted wood with sharp needlelike points at one end, the tips are presently made of plastic. In contrast to the dartboards made of wood or cork, the new computer dartboards are made of synthetic material with tiny holes that the darts intersect. These electronic dartboards are computer efficient, and they can track and record scores. Men and women alike find darts to be an exciting, entertaining game.

THE NEXT STEP

Celebrate the new millennium by investing in a dartboard. Prices can run from forty dollars up to several hundred dollars. Then call some of your friends and have a year 2000 tournament.

CATEGORIZE THE BOOKS AND CDs IN YOUR LIBRARY

"I would rather have a good plan today than a perfect plan two weeks from now."

—General George S. Patton

52

Unless you're the exception to the rule, there's probably neither rhyme nor reason to the arrangement of your books and CDs.

As you begin a new millennium, make a firm resolution to categorize your books and CDs.

Arranging your books can be done in a couple of ways, either personal categories that you create and name or by using the Dewey decimal classification. The easiest way I have found is to compile a list of ten to twenty category subjects such as novels, children, reference, religion, politics, self-help, family, home improvement, business, finance, etc.

A suggestion for keeping books in similar categories together is to use a colored sticky dot affixed to the bottom of the spine of each book. Each color indicates a category. See the on-line reference below for help with the Dewey decimal system.

Compact discs can be categorized in the same way, using a colored sticky dot affixed to each jewel case. Categories could include jazz, popular, country-western, rock, heavy metal, children, Christmas, etc. Another suggestion is to purchase leather-like vinyl organizers with plastic sleeves and discard the jewel boxes, possibly using an organizer for each category. Either way, you'll know what you have and be able to find it in the year 2000.

FYI

Two helpful books: *Organize Your Home* and *Organize Your Office* – both by Eisenberg and Kelly.

CLEAN YOUR CLOSETS AND DONATE YOUR OLD CLOTHES

> "It is more blessed to give than to receive."
>
> —Acts 20:35 NIV

53

When my wife and I decided to relocate, it meant the inevitable—selling our house and moving. After seventeen years and four kids, we had in reality accumulated a mountain of unused, retired, shrunk, and even new-but-unworn clothing, not to mention accumulated junk of every size and shape. The work of sorting and packing, though at times sad, was the beginning of some unexpected blessings.

I decided to be a good citizen and take the clothes to a second-hand store. From information that I had heard about making tax-deductible donations, I checked with the store to see if this was true. They confirmed that it was and provided me with a form to be filled out for tax purposes. The result—I received over $700 in tax deductions. But the real winner was the store, which received almost $4,000 in salable clothing and other goods that we had amassed over the years.

One of the nicest things that you could do for others in the year 2000 is to clean out your closets and donate those extra clothes. Make this a priority on your "to do" list and receive a double blessing. Not only will you get a tax deduction, but you will be assisting those who are less fortunate.

FYI

Check out the Goodwill Industries Web site:
http://www.goodwill.org.

BUY FOUR TICKETS TO THE SYMPHONY—NOT JUST TWO

"The song is ended but the melody lingers on."

—Anonymous

54

Someone told me long ago that when you buy tickets for a symphony or stage play, always buy two extra tickets. If it's enjoyable for two people, usually a husband and wife, it's double the fun when you invite friends to accompany and share it with you.

Many cities provide season subscription plans for symphonies and stage plays. If you sign up for a subscription program, you will get a substantial discount in the price of tickets, and that will make taking two friends along more affordable.

Involving friends in cultural events is a wonderful way to strengthen current friendships. Inviting neighbors to share the symphony with you is a splendid method to get to know them better. Maybe there's a young couple at work or living nearby who is struggling financially and needs encouragement from others. They would especially appreciate an invitation to a cultural event.

Your guests may have some special comments or knowledge about the symphony's selections that add to the occasion. You may also find later that you associate the musical selections that the symphony played at that event with the friends who accompanied you.

THE NEXT STEP

Make definite plans to attend the symphony during the new millennium, and be sure to take some friends with you.

SEND FLOWERS JUST TO SAY "I LOVE YOU"

"When a man brings his wife flowers for no reason—he'd better have one."

—Anonymous

55

We chuckle at this old saying because people often do use flowers to apologize for an argument or to cover an indiscretion, but a person doesn't have to be in trouble to have flowers delivered.

You don't have to wait for an anniversary or a birthday to give flowers. Flowers can be sent for no other reason than simply to say, "I love you!" Spouses may always be the initial recipient of flowers, but floral arrangements can and should be sent to all your loved ones—children, parents, grandparents, a close friend, a special teacher, or a coworker who needs some extra encouragement.

Be creative as to how and where you send them. Why have the flowers delivered to one's home when they will probably get more "buzz" and plaudits at work? Interestingly, men are just as thrilled to get flowers at work as women. It lets their colleagues know how much a loved one cares for them. Sending flowers to another person is one of the nicest demonstrations of love that you can offer.

During the year 2000, commit yourself to sending flowers to a loved one for no other reason than to say, "I love you." That's a message that is always welcome.

FYI

 A wonderful resource for flowers on the Internet is www.proflowers.com.

BUY A BOOK
FOR THE PUBLIC LIBRARY

"Books are the quietest and most constant of friends; they are the most accessible and wisest of counselors, and the most patient of teachers."

—Charles William Eliot

56

One of the favorite sayings of one of my college professors was, "Sell your bed and buy a book." He felt that books were so important for motivation, inspiration, stimulation, and knowledge that he continually emphasized buying books.

My old professor may have carried it a bit too far; yet, what he was trying to emphasize to his students was the importance of having good books around you at all times.

Libraries are in the business of acquiring books for the public's use. The biggest problem is that they don't have enough "beds to sell." If a library's budget for new books in one year is $50,000, that budget will allow a purchase of only about 5,000 books. To most people that quantity seems like a lot of new books, and it is to a small library. But when you consider the growth in potential library users and in the number of new books publishers release in a year, 5,000 new books added to the library is almost inconsequential.

Libraries never have enough money for new books. They always come out on the short end of city council budgets. During the year 2000, why don't you sell your bed and buy a book? Even if you don't sell your bed, make a personal commitment to purchase a book for your nearest public library.

FYI

Book resource: http://www.acses.com.

SIGN UP FOR
BALLROOM DANCE LESSONS

"Come and trip it as ye go,
On the light fantastic toe."

—John Milton

57

"I signed my wife and myself up for ballroom dance lessons a few weeks ago and we just graduated. We really had a ball, at least I did, and now I'm ready to get down and boogie."

Let me confess that I was a little shocked when I heard our pastor introduce his sermon with this statement and then give a demonstration. To this day I don't remember the point of the sermon, but I do remember his talking about the great fun he had taking ballroom dance lessons with his wife.

Most wives would be thrilled if their husbands would take the initiative to sign up for dance lessons—and hopefully, the reverse would be true. As you know, there are numerous opportunities for dancing—weddings, parties, clubs, cruises, to name a few. But if you're embarrassed and unsure, you'll probably sit on the sidelines and watch. Why not get involved? Think of the thrill of saying to your spouse, "Let's go dancing tonight."

The benefits are many: exercise, relaxation, romantic stimulus, making new friends, increasing your self-confidence, and having a new form of entertainment. Plus, you'll learn to foxtrot, rumba, waltz, tango, cha-cha, and swing.

This is the year to try something new. Don't be bashful—take the plunge. Sign up for ballroom dance lessons during the new millennium and make the year 2000 a year to remember.

Check out the Arthur Murray dance studio
Web site for more information:
http://www.dancetonight.com.

101 Things To Do In The Year 2000

TAKE A RIDE
IN A HOT-AIR BALLOON

"It's better to be a lion for a day than a sheep all your life."

—Sister Elizabeth Kenny

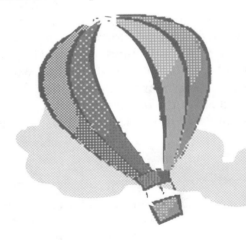

58

Have you ever fantasized about floating over the earth in a hot-air balloon? Would you like to be able to look down on the majesty of the planet? To fly with the eagles? To be able to reach out and touch the treetops? To witness life from an elevated viewpoint? You can do all this in calm serenity on a balloon flight.

Having a 360-degree panoramic view of the earth is an experience never to be forgotten. Even people who have a fear of heights have said they were amazed that riding in a balloon didn't bother them.

Be adventuresome in the year 2000. Try something that will stimulate you down to the tips of your toes. Investigate the possibility of taking a hot-air balloon ride as a new millennium celebration.

The Balloonists' Prayer

The wind has welcomed you with softness.
The sun has blessed you with warm hands.
You have flown so high and so well
That God has joined you in laughter,
And set you gently back again
Into the loving arms of mother earth.

Information on where balloon rides are offered is easy to find on the Internet. Two noteworthy sites to investigate are http://www.launch.net/ and http://www.hot-airballoons.com/ (where you can have the experience of taking a cyber-ride).

VOLUNTEER TO COLLECT
MONEY FOR A GOOD CAUSE

"Sometimes give your services for nothing, calling to mind a previous benefaction or present satisfaction."

—Hippocrates

59

"**A**nother plea for money? Give me a break. Don't you have anything better to do with your time?"

That's a typical response of many people when they are asked for a donation to a charity. But let's put it into a different perspective. What if there were no one asking for money? What if there were no organizations calling, knocking on doors, and sending requests in the mail? What if raising money for birth defects, cancer, diabetes, MS, and muscular dystrophy were outlawed? We might think, *Good. Those organizations are just a pain in the neck anyway.*

But we're not talking about organizations; we're talking about the many hundreds of thousands of lives that have been improved and spared because concerned individuals recognized a need to raise money for research.

I must confess that I was one of those who complained when asked to contribute a dime or dollar for every mile walked—until I discovered that I had diabetes. Having a currently incurable disease certainly motivates one to get involved.

You can be a pledge-taker, doorknocker, walker, or volunteer coordinator. Your charitable work can be as private as mailing out contribution requests or as public as actually participating in a walk-a-thon.

Make the year 2000 a year filled with good deeds. Become a volunteer for a specific good cause.

FYI

Web sites on charities: http://www.guidestar.org and http://www.give.org.

MAKE A LIST
OF ALL YOUR BLESSINGS

When upon life's billows
   you are tempest tossed,
When you are discouraged,
   thinking all is lost,
Count your many
   blessings, name them
   one by one,
And it will
   surprise you
   what the Lord
   hath done.

—from the hymn "Count Your Many
Blessings" by J. Oatman Jr.

60

In the 1954 movie classic *White Christmas*, Bing Crosby recommends counting your blessings instead of sheep as a reliable cure for worry and insomnia.

Counting blessings as a means of warding off insomnia may or may not work, but you should still make counting your blessings a regular habit. It's easy to forget the many ways you have been blessed. During the year 2000, make a deliberate decision to sit down and assemble a list of the endless number of blessings that have come your way. Your compiled list will have dozens, even hundreds, of blessings noted—a wonderful spouse or significant other, children, grandchildren, wonderful friends, a job that you love, your health, a place to stay warm and dry during bad weather, the freedom of speech, the freedom to worship as you wish, and on and on.

Even though bumps in the road may arise along life's path, they are interspersed with innumerable blessings from above.

FYI

A great book: *Basket of Blessings: 31 Days to a More Grateful Heart* by Karen O'Connor.

SURPRISE YOUR FRIENDS
WITH A BIRTHDAY CARD

"Age is opportunity no less
Than youth itself, though
   in another dress,
And as the evening
   twilight fades
   away,
The sky is filled
   with stars
   invisible by
   day."

—"Old Age" by Henry Wadsworth Longfellow

61

An important maxim: One of the finest ways to honor an individual and to show that you especially care for that person is to remember his or her birthday.

Some people say, as they get older, they don't like all the hoopla and celebration associated with birthdays. But is there anyone who doesn't want to be remembered? Whether you are five or seventy-five, it's a boost to know people are thinking of you for no other reason than that it is the date of your birth. Probably the saddest people in the world are those who had a birthday and no one remembered—no cards, no visits, and no calls.

A noteworthy project for the year 2000 is to begin compiling the birth dates of as many friends, coworkers, and acquaintances as possible. When a birthday rolls around, be prepared to send out that birthday greeting. Here are some additional ideas:

- Always have a small pad available to jot down names and birthdays.

- As you get to know a person or client, tell him or her you are collecting birth dates and ask them for theirs.

- Use a computer calendar to simplify the work and make it perpetual.

A wonderful service on the Internet that will stimulate more birthday ideas is found at http://www.birthdaylist.com/.

READ THE BOOK OF
ECCLESIASTES

"There is a time for everything, and a season for every activity under heaven."

—Ecclesiastes 3:1 NIV

62

The book of Ecclesiastes is filled with pithy proverbs and epigrammatic statements. Such assertions as "A good name is better than fine perfume" (Ecclesiastes 7:1) and "Whoever loves money never has money enough" (Ecclesiastes 5:10) are from the lips of King Solomon, purported to be the wisest man in the world and the author of Ecclesiastes.

Even though you don't have the surpassing wealth and the impressive wisdom of King Solomon, maybe you can find some analogies between his life in biblical times and your life in the world today.

- Solomon reflected back on his life and was not overly delighted with what he saw.

- Solomon tried to analyze what brings happiness and fulfillment and was stymied.

- Solomon considered the future and how life should be lived. His final conclusion is found in Ecclesiastes 12:13–14 NIV, which says, "Fear God and keep his commandments, for this is the whole duty of man."

Whether you've read the Bible or not, resolve that during this coming new year you will read the book of Ecclesiastes. Put that resolve on your "to do" list for 2000. You will find this Old Testament book to be fascinating and contemporary. Read it in comparison with your life at this point in time.

A probing book proving an overview of Ecclesiastes: *Soul Search* by Ricker and Pitkin.

101 Things To Do In The Year **2000**

SPEND A WEEKEND
AT A BED & BREAKFAST

"Wouldn't it be nice if one week of vacation seemed to last as long as one week on a diet?"

—Anonymous

63

One Christmas our four children, instead of buying individual presents for my wife and me, pooled their Christmas resources and treated us to a weekend at a bed and breakfast. Not only was it one of the nicest gifts they could have given us, it was also the most delightful mini-vacation we've ever had.

If you've never been to a B&B, you're in for a treat. Quality and attention to detail are at the top of the list of most of these establishments. You may find goose down comforters, quality linens, and canopy beds with chocolates or a rose on the pillow. One thing is for sure—you can expect to be pampered. Staying at a B&B is more than just having a place to lay your head at night—it is truly an unforgettable experience.

With over 15,000 bed and breakfasts across America, they're easy to find and could be very close to your home. Make definite plans to celebrate the new millennium at a bed and breakfast. Decide how far you wish to travel, set a firm date, find the names of B&Bs in that area, and call for reservations. You may have to make two or three calls to find a vacancy at these very popular destinations.

FYI

One of the best sources for B&B information is found on the Internet at http://bbchannel.com/.

DRINK EIGHT GLASSES OF WATER PER DAY

"He who has health, has hope; and he who has hope, has everything."

—Arabian proverb

64

Incredible as it may seem, water is quite possibly the single most important catalyst in maintaining a healthy body, losing weight, and slowing aging.

Water accounts for about 75 percent of our weight, and it's the body's most important nutrient. Water regulates all body functions and is necessary for the removal of waste. We cannot live without it. Stranded on a desert island, we could go for weeks without food, but without water we would die within ten days.

Your goal in year 2000 is to begin drinking eight glasses of water per day. If you drink a cup of coffee in the morning, don't count it as one of the eight glasses of water. Don't count milk, tea, fruit juices, or carbonated beverages. A minimum of eight glasses of water is needed to flush the system and to retain maximum health.

Some fascinating facts:

- Some studies have shown that drinking cold water may actually help burn calories.
- When you don't drink water, your body has a tendency to retain water as a safety measure. Result: it may show up as excess weight.
- A paradox: To get rid of excess water, you must drink more water.

FYI

Good information can be found at The Waterworks: http://capestorm.com/water.htm.

MAKE THE GOLDEN RULE YOUR PERSONAL LIFE PHILOSOPHY

"Always do for other people everything you want them to do for you."

—Matthew 7:12 GOD'S WORD

65

Even in the touchiest situations, my friend Gail always goes out of her way to treat people kindly and with understanding. One might think she deals gently with people because she's a weak person. Not so. Gail has a strong personality. She simply exemplifies the Golden Rule. People highly respect her because she treats others like she herself wants to be treated.

Gail seems to be the exception in this matter. Most of us talk a good game when it comes to the Golden Rule, but we often practice a double standard. The Golden Rule applies to everyone else, not us.

If you want people to treat you kindly, you must treat them kindly. If you want other people to understand your feelings, you must attempt to understand theirs. If you want people to speak well of you, you must speak well of other people. If you want people to give you a hardy pat on the back, you must be willing to do the same to them. Just because you memorized the Golden Rule as a child doesn't make it a reality in your life.

To paraphrase this New Testament maxim: "I will treat you as I want to be treated. Please treat me as you yourself want to be treated." You'll discover as Gail has that this takes a great deal of strength. You may even be misunderstood by those who don't observe your behavior for very long. But you will feel the strength of love growing inside you, and you will soon see others treating you just as kindly as you treat them.

THE NEXT STEP

Determine today that in the year 2000 you will make the Golden Rule your personal philosophy.

LEARN TO USE E-MAIL

> "Whoopee. I did it. I'm now
> on-line with e-mail."
>
> —Connie Havens

66

The excited comments were from a friend, a grandmother, and a computer novice. It took her over a year to get the courage just to sit down at the computer, let alone use it on her own. But when she finally got on-line by herself, it was like the weight of the world had been lifted. She had faced up to the enemy, engaged him in battle—and she had come out the winner!

This grandmother is typical of so many people who, for the first time, are becoming acquainted with on-line communication via the computer. For some reason, this little machine with the ironclad logic generates an inner fear in many people. In some cases, it's a fear of the unknown, and in others it's a fear of doing damage to the machine so that it will never work again.

E-mail is the new, quick, and wonderful way of communicating with family, friends, or customers throughout the world. In a typical day, I receive up to fifty e-mails, including messages from England, Thailand, Mexico, and Hawaii.

If there is a computer in your home and you're not yet set up on e-mail, make this one of your top priorities for the year 2000. The yellow pages of your phone directory have many listings for providers of this service. You will find the cost very low and the return very high for most of them.

This technology has opened a brand new world of communication where you can share instantly with friends and relatives, no matter how far away. Believe me, you'll be hooked when you get hooked up to e-mail.

FYI

Book: *Email for Dummies*, edited by Levine. Good, free e-mail site: http://hotmail.com.

101 Things To Do In The Year 2000

BUY A COPY
OF *THE GIVING TREE*

"Behold, I do not give
lectures or a little charity.
When I give I give myself."

—Walt Whitman

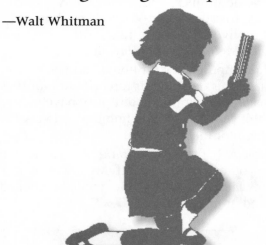

67

I have a hard time reading Shel Silverstein's *The Giving Tree* without choking up. It is one of the finest stories ever written for children. It demonstrates to children and adults alike that to love is to give. It provides the perfect demonstration of selflessness.

The story is about the transformation of a young boy who always takes and takes and an apple tree that continually gives and gives. As a young child, the boy loves the tree. He is constantly playing on it and around it. As he grows older he doesn't come to the tree much anymore. When he does visit, he always seems to need something.

Because the tree is unselfish and loves the boy dearly, it gives the boy what it has—fruit, branches, and trunk. In other words, the tree gives its entire self to the boy. The story instructs us well with the message that the one who loves is always a giver.

If you, your children, or your grandchildren have never been introduced to *The Giving Tree*, let me suggest that you hasten to a bookstore right now, and bring home a life-changing book. Not only will you be personally touched, but it will also become the basis of an object lesson in the new millennium—the lifelong value of giving.

Internet sources for purchasing your copy of *The Giving Tree*: http://amazon.com or http://barnesandnoble.com.

SUBSCRIBE TO A
WEEKLY NEWSMAGAZINE

"All I know is what I read
in the papers."

—Will Rogers

68

Recently while sitting around the lunch table at work, someone made a comment about the latest governmental scandal. Two of the six people at the table pleaded ignorance. They had no idea what their coworkers were talking about, even though the story of the scandal had received prime-time coverage on TV the night before. It was hard to believe that one-third of the group was unaware of what was happening.

To extrapolate and say that one-third of the American people have no knowledge of current events is certainly not a perfect poll, but it may be relatively close. As citizens we need to be cognizant of what is happening in the world. One of the best ways to stay up-to-date on the ever-changing news is to scan a weekly digest of current events. There are numerous newsmagazines available, but the three primary ones are *Newsweek*, *Time*, and *U.S. News & World Report*. These magazines deal with current national and international news and politics, but they also touch on every current news subject imaginable—health issues, computers, sports, movies, books, women's issues, men's issues, and investments.

The coming new millennium will bring about tremendous changes at home and internationally. All of us need to stay updated as best we can on the latest news. Subscribing to a newsmagazine may be the easiest way. Make this one of the items you plan to do in the year 2000.

FYI

Internet source for news:
http://www.foxnews.com.

101 Things To Do In The Year **2000**

WALK BAREFOOT IN THE OCEAN WITH YOUR SPOUSE

> "A thing of beauty is a joy forever."
>
> —John Keats

69

It's a marvelous experience to walk barefoot on the edge of a lake or stream. There's something very relaxing about the feel of sand forcing itself through your toes, the cool water engulfing your feet and ankles, the ripple of the current, and the breaking of miniwaves on the shore. Calmness overtakes you as you see fish jump or turtles sunning themselves on a log.

As nice as a lake is, walking barefoot in the great expanse of the ocean is better. It's thrilling to stride along in the Atlantic Ocean on the New England coast where the first settlers steered their ships to shore. It's delightful in a different way to walk in the waters of the Pacific off the shores of California. And few things can compare to the resplendent majesty of the setting sun across the waves of the ocean as you walk along the beach.

But all these experiences at water's edge have even more beauty and meaning when they are shared with your spouse. Holding hands, the two of you will be drawn closer as you walk together in this most plentiful of all natural elements.

THE NEXT STEP

Set aside a day to walk in the ocean or a nearby lake with your loved one in the year 2000. The two of you will find it an exhilarating experience.

101 Things To Do In The Year 2000

TEST YOUR BIBLE KNOWLEDGE

"See what God has done!"

—Numbers 23:23 NIV

70

OK, let's check your knowledge of the Bible!

- Who lived in the belly of a great fish for three days?
- Whose voice did Moses clearly hear coming from a burning bush?
- Is the Old Testament longer or shorter than the New Testament?

The Bible continues to be the national number-one bestseller. Almost every family in America has at least one copy of the Bible in their home. The question is not whether you have a copy of the Bible, the question is how much of the Bible do you know? Many people, no doubt, feel somewhat like Mark Twain, who said he wasn't bothered by the things in the Bible that he didn't understand—it was the things in the Bible that he did understand that bothered him.

Determine during this new millennial year to become acquainted with the stories, the history, and the facts of the Bible. One of the best and most entertaining methods for checking your knowledge is to make use of *Bible Brain Quest*. Almost every key story and fact in the Bible is covered in this unique quiz and learning guide.

THE NEXT STEP

Add the *Bible Brain Quest* to your year 2000 buying list and test your Bible knowledge.

101 Things To Do In The Year 2000

VISIT A NATIONAL HISTORIC SITE

What's Past Is Prologue

—William Shakespeare

71

A cartoon shows two dogs talking to each other. One dog comments to the other, "So many fire hydrants and so little time."

That is how we Americans should react when it comes to reliving our national history—so many historical sites to see, so much of history to experience, and so little time. Our nation is filled with sensational historical sites to visit, but I'll mention just four that are representative of other great historical sites.

- Williamsburg, Virginia, is a fun place for the whole family. The community involves the visitors in events of early American history. You will be more than just a spectator.

- Boston, Massachusetts, is perfect for the history buff. The two-and-a-half mile Freedom Trail allows you firsthand experience of America's early history.

- San Antonio, Texas, is best known for the Alamo and Davey Crockett.

- Washington, D.C., is the home of our national Capitol. You can stop by the White House, meander through the Smithsonian Institution, ascend the Washington Monument, and drop in at the National Air and Space Museum.

Get a taste of history and a new appreciation for the United States of America by making plans to visit one of the great historical sites during the year 2000.

Two excellent Web site sources for national park information are www.americanparks.com/locator.htm and http://usparks.miningco.com/mbody.htm.

VOLUNTEER AT A HOMELESS SHELTER OR SOUP KITCHEN

"A hungry people listens not to reason, nor cares for justice, nor is bent by any prayers."

—Seneca the Younger

72

It was Jesus who said: "For the poor always ye have with you" (John 12:8 KJV).

Simply because Jesus confirmed that the poor will always be a part of society doesn't mean we can accept that as a fact of life and move on. For it was Jesus who also admonished society with these words, "For I was an hungered, and ye gave me no meat: I was thirsty, and ye gave me no drink: I was a stranger, and ye took me not in: naked, and ye clothed me not" (Matthew 25:42–43 KJV).

Rabbi Kroloff shares some interesting insights about the poor in his book, *54 Ways You Can Help the Homeless*. Here are just a few:

- One out of four homeless people is a war veteran.
- One out of four homeless people is a child.
- The number of homeless on any one night during the year is probably over three million.
- Many homeless people have completed high school; some have attended college and even graduate school.

As you enter into the year 2000, don't forget those less fortunate than yourself. Resolve to be a volunteer throughout the year, not just at Thanksgiving or Christmas when volunteers are abundant.

FYI

Contact the Web site for Volunteers of America:
http//www.voa.org.

101 Things To Do In The Year 2000

REVISIT YOUR OLD HIGH SCHOOL

"I have never let my schooling interfere with my education."

—Mark Twain

73

Thinking of high school brings back mountains of memories. It was a place of learning, but it was more, much more. Probably no experience in life was filled with higher highs and lower lows. Few things can compare to some of the initial events from this time of life—the first date, the first kiss, the posted list announcing that you had made the team, the prom, the ball games, the favorite teachers, and of course the close friends. School memories also bring to mind the anxieties of dating, conflicts with teachers and friends, and the ever-elusive quest to determine who you were and what life had to offer. For some of you reading this page, high school may only be five or ten years back down the road. But for me, high school is forty years in the past; yet, certain events are as clear as what happened yesterday.

Would you like to recreate some of your great memories? Resolve during the year 2000 to return to your high school. Your favorite teachers may be gone. Your friends will be gone (unless they are now teachers). But the memories will still be there. What a great way to reminisce!

You may be lucky enough to have a class reunion in 2000. As for me, I look forward to celebrating the fortieth year since high school graduation by visiting my old school.

Plan your trip with a map:
http//www.mapsonus.com.

GIVE ONE SINCERE
COMPLIMENT EVERY DAY

"I can live for two months
on a good compliment."

—Mark Twain

74

Few things that you can do for another person have a more positive, invigorating result than giving a sincere compliment. Do these examples give you any ideas?

"I've never had a neighbor who is so willing to help out when I'm in need." "You have such a positive attitude—it's contagious."

"I love your new hairstyle. You look absolutely terrific."

"Aren't you wearing new glasses? The shape of the frames is just right for you."

Consider how you react and the long-term effect after you receive a *specific, sincere compliment*. These last three words should be your guide as you remember to praise others:

- Specific—exact, particular, precise. Something definite and detailed.
- Sincere—honest, genuine, bona fide. Free from hypocrisy.
- Compliment—praise and honor. An expression of approval and appreciation.

A sincere, specific compliment stands in contrast to flattery that praises another person but is replete with hypocrisy.

THE NEXT STEP

During the year 2000 resolve to give at least one sincere, specific compliment each day of the year.

BREAK ONE BAD HABIT DURING THE YEAR

"I can handle pain unless it hurts."

—Anonymous

75

Habits, both good and bad, affect who you are. Drinking, smoking, and biting one's nails come to mind when bad habits are mentioned. But so is overeating, procrastination, inconsiderate driving, and laziness. Is there a bad habit that you'd like to break?

If you want to break a habit, you need a plan. Here are some questions to consider:

1. What habit do you most want to change?
2. What problems are created by this habit?
3. What are the advantages and benefits of breaking this habit?
4. What difficult situations might weaken your resolve?
5. What are some alternatives that you can substitute for the bad habit?
6. What kind of reasonable date will you set for achieving your goal?

Work through this list and then make a resolution to conquer your bad habit. Studies show that it takes about twenty-one days to establish or change a habit.

THE NEXT STEP

Make a public declaration that you're going to break a specific bad habit in the year 2000—and then go for it!

101 Things To Do In The Year 2000

MAKE PLANS TO BE AN ORGAN DONOR

"If you want to lift yourself up, lift up someone else."

—Booker T. Washington

76

I've recently made the decision that when I die I would like to donate my body for medical research and transplants.

Currently, I'm working with an individual who undergoes kidney dialysis treatments regularly. As I heard his story, I was touched by a real need. I've since acquired my donor card over the Internet. The next step will be to have my desires noted on my driver's license. And the final step will be receiving my family's approval. If I don't have their approval, my desire for organ donation will be of no avail when I die. At that point, they have the final say-so.

Organ donations and transplants save lives. Each day across the nation about fifty people receive organ transplants, yet many more die because there are not enough organs to go around. The more donors there are, the more lives that can be saved.

- Your heart could beat for someone else.
- Your lungs could breathe for someone else.
- Your kidneys could free two people from dialysis.
- Your liver could save the life of one awaiting a transplant.
- Your corneas could give sight to two people.

Make the year 2000 a notable year, the year that you decided to become an organ donor. This is a tough decision, but it's a decision that can save lives.

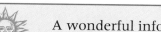

A wonderful information resource, as well as a donor card, is available at http://organdonor.gov.

SPEND TIME IN A CEMETERY READING EPITAPHS

"Under the sod and under
the trees
Lies the body of Jonathan
Pease.
He is not here, there's only
the pod:
Pease shelled
out and went to
God."

77

It's fun to laugh at the sayings on some of those old tombstones. The early dates are mind-boggling because these people lived so long ago. But walking through a graveyard is not like a walk in the park. There is something about walking through a cemetery that makes one realize life is not forever.

If you ever visit New England, you might stop by one of the old cemeteries in that area. Because most of the cities in that part of the country were founded in the seventeenth and eighteenth centuries, cemeteries are much more prevalent. Recently, when visiting the Old North Church graveyard in Boston, I found the tombstone of a relative who died in 1632. Unbelievable!

Even if you can't go to New England, you can visit a nearby graveyard. Some of the most interesting ones may be the smaller sites out in the countryside. Tracing a family's lineage through tombstones is also interesting.

During the millennial year, visit a cemetery and reflect on the dates, the epitaphs, and on life itself. You might also look for newer tombstones just erected in the year 2000. Life goes on.

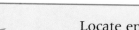

FYI

Locate epitaphs on the Internet:
http://www.netins.net/showcase/kadinger/
anthology.htm.

LEARN TO PLAY
A MUSICAL INSTRUMENT

> "Music is the universal
> language of mankind."
>
> —Henry Wadsworth Longfellow

78

I've always wanted to play a musical instrument. I have envied my friends who could play the piano and guitar. It wasn't until I got to college that I had the chance to take piano lessons. After twelve exciting lessons (at least I thought they were exciting), my teacher became extremely ill and my days of learning to play the piano came to an end—and in case you're wondering, her sickness was not caused by my piano playing.

Many of you reading this book have musical talent, but chances to learn an instrument passed you by. There is good news for you. Modern technology has made it easier than ever.

- There are several computer software programs now on the market that will turn your computer into a powerful piano tutor. You actually hook up a piano keyboard to your computer and almost instantly you're learning to play songs.

- An Internet resource that uses videos to teach a variety of instruments can be found at www.extelmusic.com.

- Finally, if you want to turn your computer keyboard into a piano keyboard and make beautiful music, contact Sweet Little Piano at www.ronimusic.com/sweet_pi.htm.

Turn over a new leaf with the dawning of a new millennium. Become a musical connoisseur.

THE NEXT STEP

Commit yourself to learning a musical instrument and discover that playing music is one of the most relaxing, satisfying activities that you can do during the year 2000.

SEND ONE THANK YOU CARD EVERY WEEK

> "Gratitude is not only the greatest of virtues, but the parent of all the others."
>
> —Cicero

79

Think about it! There are few things that you appreciate more than receiving a thank you note. Imagine a salesperson sitting down and sending you a thank you note after your car purchase or a parent sending you a note of thanks for coaching the soccer team or a coworker sending you a thank you card for listening when he or she needed someone to talk to. How do you feel when you receive such a note?

For many people, writing or sending a thank you card is a waste of time. "Why should I send a card of thanks? They know I appreciate what they did." It would be funny if it weren't so sad—the same people who don't take the time to send thank you cards sure seem to enjoy receiving them.

Why not make a list of people who have meant or currently mean a great deal to you? People who have gone out of their way for you at work, the service station, the insurance office, or the grocery store. Then each week during the year 2000, send a note or card to one of these people and surprise them by saying "thank you."

FINAL THOUGHT

Important maxim: People always remember a thank you note long after they forget exactly what they did to deserve it.

WORK TO CONQUER ONE OF
YOUR PRINCIPAL FEARS

"You gain strength, courage, and confidence by every experience in which you really stop to look fear in the face. You must do the thing which you think you cannot do."

—Eleanor Roosevelt

80

According to specialists, there are more than two hundred different kinds of phobias. There are phobias of cleanliness, leaving home, being alone, being in a crowd, being on an elevator, being on a subway, being in water, and on and on. It's very common to hear of someone who is afraid of flying, or of heights, or of public speaking.

In a sense, fear acts like a big brother to protect you from harm, such as when the big Doberman approaches, fear is there to say "be careful." But big brother can also get in your way by making you miss opportunities. Whether you have a giant phobia or a tiny fear, each one is very real.

Prevention magazine offers some secrets to help make fear disappear:

- Fear is erased by knowledge. One of the main components of fear is uncertainty.
- Training breeds confidence. Learn how to do what frightens you.
- Talking helps. Suppressing your fears doesn't work.
- It's okay to get help. Talk to a doctor or psychologist and get needed help.

Whatever your principal fear, dedicate yourself to conquering it in the new millennium. This is a project that may need work throughout the year 2000.

THE NEXT STEP

 An excellent resource book is *Anxiety and Panic Attacks: The Five-Point Life-Plus Program for Conquering Fear* by Robert Handly and Pauline Neff.

VISIT PRISONERS IN A LOCAL JAIL

"Then the King will say to those on his right, 'Come, you who are blessed by my Father. . . . I was in prison and you came to visit me.'"

—Matthew 25:34-36 NIV

81

Close to 1.5 million people are incarcerated in United States prisons today. Some interesting facts about prisoners:

- Most inmates spend twenty to twenty-two hours a day confined in their cells.

- Experts estimate that at least half of 1 percent of the current inmate population is innocent.

- AIDS in state and federal prisons is six times higher than in the population at large.

Possibly you're saying, "Interesting facts. But why should I visit a prison?" First, many prisoners have neither personal contact nor correspondence while they are in prison. These are lonely people, disillusioned with society and, undoubtedly, very resentful. Kindness and concern can break down these damaging attitudes. A visit from the outside says, "I care about you." Since most prisoners will eventually be released, your visit could help, in a small way, to prepare them for their return to society.

Second, many of these men and women have families on the outside—families that are struggling just to have enough food and clothing. You may learn of opportunities to help an inmate's family.

THE NEXT STEP

Visiting a prisoner in the year 2000 may not excite you, but it's needed. Check with your local church. Many have prison visitation ministries already established, and they will welcome your participation.

INVITE THE MAYOR OR SCHOOL SUPERINTENDENT TO DINNER

"May our house always be too small to hold all our friends."

—Myrtle Reed

82

Inviting some of the most visible leaders in your community to dinner may be a little presumptuous. Without a doubt, issuing the invitation is going to take a little grit, a little nerve, and a lot of courage, but they can't do anything worse than say "no."

Both the mayor and the superintendent are concerned about what you're thinking on a wide range of issues. These leaders are not only influenced by public opinion, but they are also looking for public approval for their policies.

Being together for a meal provides the perfect forum to find out what's happening in the community. You might even question them about:

- What do we need to do to get more money allocated to the public library for new books?
- Was the one million dollars really necessary to revamp the city jail?
- Why do real estate taxes keep going up year after year?
- Is it true that kids are bringing dangerous weapons to the schools? Would a metal detector be a deterrent?

THE NEXT STEP

Drawing on all your bravery, give the mayor or superintendent a call and invite them to a meal in the year 2000. This could be one of the more memorable occurrences during this new millennial year.

177

101 Things To Do In The Year 2000

ORDER PIZZA
FOR ALL YOUR COWORKERS

"Gratitude is the fairest
blossom which springs
from the soul."

—Henry Ward Beecher

83

It's safe to say that most people have a hunger to be appreciated and that usually this hunger goes unsatisfied. As the year 2000 rolls around, be the one person in your department or on your shift who attempts to satisfy this hunger for appreciation—and for pizza.

Pick a specific day and announce that you're ordering pizza for everyone for lunch and paying for it. This works best if you have some specific reason you can name, but be sure you let your coworkers know how much you appreciate their support. You don't have to be the boss to instigate an appreciation day; you can be on the bottom rung of the ladder. It makes no difference.

Your goal on this appreciation day is to show your coworkers that you, personally, esteem them. You can do that with cheese, sausage, pepperoni, and vegetables on thick or thin crust!

This little year 2000 "thank you" party may cost you thirty or forty dollars, but it could be the best money you've ever spent. And sometime in the future it might come back to you multiplied many times over.

FYI

Papa John's Pizza is growing fast:
http://www.papajohns.com.

ORGANIZE A NEIGHBORHOOD BLOCK PARTY

"If we would build on a sure foundation in friendship, we must love friends for their sake rather than for our own."

—Charlotte Brontë

84

I have a great desire to get to know my neighbors, but I let my personal agenda and maybe a little timidity seem to rule. My wife suggested we think about organizing a block party, so that's one of our big projects for the summer of 2000.

If you're not familiar with a neighborhood block party, it's an outdoor event for everyone living on a street or in a well-defined area. Usually the street is blocked off for games and contests and a shared meal. It's an enjoyable way to get to know your neighbors, boost community spirit, and have fun all at the same time. Be sure to check with your city offices for approval.

Here's a list of ideas and considerations:

- Contact every home in the neighborhood to find volunteers to help plan and organize the party.
- Set a date and time for the block party.
- Determine expenses and, if necessary, decide how to collect contributions.
- Decide what type of food and beverages will be served.
- Plan a variety of activities and games for both children and adults around the theme of the new millennium.
- Finally, be absolutely certain that all the neighbors get an invitation and respond for the big "Year 2000 Neighborhood Bash."

FINAL THOUGHT

Your neighborhood block party may be such a success that it will happen again in 2001!

GIVE AN "I LOVE YOU" CARD
TO YOUR SPOUSE MONTHLY

"There is no more lovely, friendly, and charming relationship, communion, or company than a good marriage."

—Martin Luther

85

Each and every month during the year 2000 give an "I love you" card to your spouse. Make it a fun experience that neither of you will forget. Go shopping with thirty or forty dollars and plan to buy most of the "I love you" cards at one time—though you may want to buy certain, specific cards around a seasonal celebration.

Be creative and make the presentation of each card an extra special occasion. You might consider some of these ideas:

- Mail the card to arrive at work or at home.
- Take your spouse to a fine restaurant and present the card there.
- Have it tied to "I Love You" balloons and have the balloons delivered.
- Present the card at breakfast and include inside a pair of tickets to some special event, such as a musical or play.
- Make reservations at an area Bed & Breakfast and have the card waiting for your spouse when you arrive.
- Place it under his or her pillow with a gift of some new sleepwear.
- Attach his or her favorite cologne to the card and set it in a conspicuous place.

FINAL THOUGHT

Plan to have fun presenting the "I love you" cards as you enjoy the year 2000 together.

SEND A NOTE OF LOVE
TO YOUR CHILDREN MONTHLY

"Children need love,
especially when they do not
deserve it."

—Harold S. Hubert

86

Authorities tell us that the number one fear among young people is the fear of rejection. They fear rejection by their peers, and they fear rejection by their parents. Experts say that parental rejection is one of the strongest predictors of delinquent behavior. Statistics indicate that the rejected person is more likely to become a violent criminal.

Richard Johnson, a family-law judge in Dallas, maintains that approximately 80 percent of the juvenile gang members he sees come from single-parent families. To the judge, the essential issue is the absence of parental love. Kids need love. They need loving reassurance. Mr. Johnson recalls that during a counseling session, one juvenile gang member was asked why he joined a gang. His answer was revealing: "No one at home ever told me that they loved me."

The primary assets parents have to give within a home are love, acceptance, and affirmation. Your children desperately need to know that you love and accept them. This is a truism whether your child is two, twenty-two, or fifty-two.

THE NEXT STEP

Dedicate yourself to sending your children a message of love and appreciation monthly during the year 2000.

101 Things To Do In The Year **2000**

DINE IN THE BEST RESTAURANT IN YOUR AREA

"One cannot think well, love well, sleep well, if one has not dined well."

—Virginia Woolf

87

There are few delights that make more of a lasting impression upon me than dining at an exquisite restaurant. A fine meal, elegant atmosphere, and superb service will be part of my conversation for weeks after the event.

My wife and I normally eat out at least once a week. Since I'm usually conscious of the cost, I often opt for a popular chain. These restaurants usually serve a good meal, and the total bill can still be in the twenty-dollar range for a couple.

Since dining in the best restaurants is one of the joys of my life, let me share some things that I do to make expensive dining a reality.

- At times, my wife and I have skipped a week or two of dining out and settled for a fast-food establishment. This has allowed us to save the extra forty to sixty dollars to be applied toward a meal in a fine restaurant.
- We have also subscribed to a two-for-one coupon book at a cost of thirty to forty dollars for the whole book. Communities often provide their own personal dining coupon book, so keep your eyes open.

These are but a few ideas for watching your pennies while you look forward to dining in the best restaurants in your area.

THE NEXT STEP

Plan to celebrate the arrival of the year 2000 by indulging yourself at an elegant place with delicious food.

EVALUATE YOUR CURRENT LIFE INSURANCE NEEDS

> "I detest life insurance agents; they always argue that I shall some day die, which is not so."
>
> —Stephen Leacock

If you listed 101 things you would like to do, I'm sure that evaluating your life insurance would not appear on the list. Thinking about life insurance is something most people avoid or wish they could avoid. It brings to mind how defenseless we are when death stands at our door. No one likes to contemplate that life will someday end.

A good life insurance policy is the cornerstone of caring for your family. Remember, life insurance is for your loved ones and not for you. You can't stick your head in the sand in hopes that death will never come or that your loved ones will have no future financial needs. If you have children and a large amount of debt such as a mortgage, and if you rely on your work income, you definitely need some life insurance. The general rule of thumb is five to ten times the insured's annual salary. That of course may vary according to your financial status, age, size of family, and other liquid assets.

In figuring your life insurance needs, you should take into account final expenses after death, such as mortgage loans, credit cards, car payments, college costs, customary living expenses, and funeral expenses. Because term insurance provides the most coverage for the least amount of money, you should investigate and consider it first.

THE NEXT STEP

During the year 2000, resolve to take the time to reevaluate your current life insurance needs. It's an important gift for your loved ones.

ARRANGE TO HAVE YOUR WILL PREPARED OR UPDATED

"Do not brag about tomorrow, because you do not know what another day may bring."

—Proverbs 27:1, GOD'S WORD

89

What happens to your property if you die without a will?

1. State law determines who gets it.
2. Your friends and relatives have to decide, and perhaps fight, among themselves to determine who gets your property.
3. The government takes your property and sells it to reduce the federal deficit.

This is the first of fifteen questions testing your knowledge about making a will in the software package *WillMaker*. Nolo Press, the publisher and manufacturer of *WillMaker* (and a specialist in legal matters), formulated these questions for their Web site at www.nolo.com.

The answer to the above question is #1. The state determines what happens to your property. The court, in the absence of a legal will and in rare circumstances, can even make the determination of who will care for your children.

If you don't have a legal will, you're like 70 percent of the population. Without a will, you haven't fully prepared your family and loved ones in the event of your death.

THE NEXT STEP

If you have not yet prepared a legal will, determine that you will have one drawn up in the year 2000. It's vitally important for your heirs.

101 Things To Do In The Year 2000

SPEND AN AFTERNOON
IN A USED-BOOK STORE

"Read the best books first,
or you may not have a
chance to read them at all."

—Henry David Thoreau

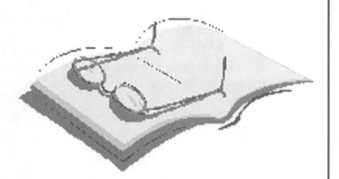

90

Most people don't realize that some of the best books written are found in used-book stores, and some of the worst books written are in today's fashionable bookstores. Our consumer-controlled society has trained us to think that the newest and the latest must be the best and the greatest, but that is a false assumption. It only takes a few minutes in a used-book store to realize that you can find hidden gems and pearls of great price, all at bargain rates.

As one of your goals for the year 2000, plan to spend an afternoon in a used-book store. If you've never been in one, you're in for a gratifying treat. If you're already a patron, you won't need any encouragement.

- You may find classics dating back into the eighteenth and nineteenth centuries.

- Used books are readily accessible and are usually in subject categories, but each store has its own unique features. The store owners also have special interests that are reflected in their collection.

- Look for good deals. Many of the books are priced at a fraction of the original price.

- Most used-book stores allow you to exchange your old books for other works on their shelves. Just think, you could walk out of the store with new (at least for you) reading material and not spend a dime.

Search here for an out-of-print book:
http://www.bookfinder.com.

TRY RISING EARLY
FOR A PERSONAL QUIET TIME

"Iron rusts from disuse; stagnant water loses its purity and in cold weather becomes frozen; even so does inaction sap the vigors of the mind."

—Leonardo da Vinci

91

I can hear your response now—"Rising early? Personal quiet time? You've got to be kidding."

Give this some thought before you say more. Each year the American Institute of Preventive Medicine issues a list of the "Top 10 Most Healthy Resolutions." Stress management is always found on this list. Stress is responsible for two-thirds of all office visits to doctors and plays a major role in the two killers, heart disease and cancer. Sixty-two percent of Americans say they experience a great deal of stress at least once a week. To manage stress the Institute recommends that people practice some type of relaxation exercise for at least twenty minutes per day.

Medical practitioners and religious leaders suggest that individuals take time each day for a personal quiet time including reflection, meditation, and prayer. Not only will this help relieve stress, but it allows you to focus on what is the most meaningful aspect of your life.

During the year 2000, set aside a minimum of one week and rise twenty minutes early for a personal quiet time. Have by your side a book of devotions and maybe a pad of paper to jot down a note or two. You may want to read a Psalm from the Bible, or you might just want to sit quietly, reflecting and praying. Twenty minutes spent this way each morning could give you twenty more years of life in the next millennium.

FYI

A great way to start the day: *Readings for Meditation and Reflection* by C. S. Lewis & Walter Hooper, ed.

101 Things To Do In The Year 2000

TRAIN TO RUN OR WALK IN A 5K ROAD RACE

"You may be disappointed if you fail, but you are doomed if you don't try."

—Beverly Sills

92

I remember my neighbor asking me if I would begin jogging with him each day. "I'll meet you tomorrow morning in front of your house at 6:15," he said one day. Thus began months of fatigue, sweating, and painful joy. My neighbor was the more experienced runner, so he helped me start slowly with an alternating pace of run, walk, run, walk, run, and walk. The half-mile eventually extended to three miles every morning. I hated getting up early every morning, I detested the pain and agony, and yet I loved every minute of it. Jogging is a strange paradox.

If jogging isn't for you, and there may be numerous reasons for this, try walking. It has similar aerobic values to jogging and is easier on your joints. In either case, you can set a goal for the year 2000 of training to run or walk in a five-kilometer road race. This suggested goal will stretch you to the limit, but there are values in this madness:

- Your overall health will improve as you train to run or walk in a race.

- Running and walking promote weight loss and improve lung capacity.

- Your mental vigor will sharpen. Many joggers report their best ideas come while running.

FINAL THOUGHT

 Training for a five-kilometer race may not be for everyone. If you have any doubt, check with your doctor. But if there are no hindrances or handicaps, you will feel like a king when you finish the race!

RESOLVE TO LEARN SOMETHING NEW EVERY DAY

"A man who carries a cat by the tail learns something he can learn in no other way."

—Mark Twain

93

If you lived a few hundred years ago, trying to learn something new every day could be quite a stretch. Science was in its infancy, books were limited, communication was extremely slow, and there was no electronic information highway.

So when the challenge comes to learn something new every day in the year 2000, the major problem may be selecting something from the great barrage of information with which you come into contact in a single day. It really is not much of challenge to find something new to learn.

Let's move the challenge up a notch and add the element of personal improvement. Commit to learn something new that will improve you as a person, as an employee, as a spouse, or as a parent. Now where do you begin?

- A great resource is the Internet. There is so much information available on-line that you could conceivably learn 365 new things in one day.

- Another great resource is self-help and inspirational books. Visit your library and bookstore regularly.

- If you want to learn some new skills as well as facts, check out the video library at www.totalmarketing.com. Thousands of learning videos are available for purchase through this resource.

THE NEXT STEP

Keep a notebook and daily jot down the one specific new thing that you learn. Make the year 2000 a great personal learning experience.

101 Things To Do In The Year 2000

GO BACK AND VISIT YOUR BIRTHPLACE

"No matter under what circumstances you leave it, home does not cease to be home. No matter how you lived there—well or poorly."

—Joseph Brodsky

was talking with a friend recently about growing up as a kid in Michigan. As we reminisced, he told me that he had grown up in Missouri but had then moved away with his family when he was about twelve years old. As we continued to talk, I detected that he had never been back to the place of his birth. *How sad*, I thought. *This man has no attachments to his early beginnings.*

As my friend and I continued to talk, I encouraged him to take the first opportunity to go back and visit his birthplace. Not only would it bless him, but it would be like finding a missing piece in the puzzle of his life.

Part of our heritage, part of who we are, is attached to where we were born and grew up. How long has it been since you've been back to your birthplace? For some it may have been only a few weeks, while for others it may have been many years or maybe never.

The year 2000 shouldn't be just for looking ahead into a new century, but it should also be a time of looking back at where you've been. The landscape, the architecture, the accents and speech patterns all had an effect on making you who you are today.

As you celebrate the new millennium, make plans to return to the place of your birth. See what you can remember. Notice how things have changed. Stop by to see an old acquaintance or two.

FINAL THOUGHT

As you reflect back on your beginnings, allow them to become a springboard for your future.

101 Things To Do In The Year 2000

LEARN ONE GREAT ILLUSION OR CARD TRICK

"Don't be afraid your life will end; be afraid that it will never begin."

—Grace Hansen

95

There's something about illusions that intrigue and mystify people, young and old. If you're looking for a way to attract an audience at a party or at work, just learn a good trick that you can present flawlessly. People will flock around you to watch. The nice thing about tricks is that anyone can learn them, and many people can make use of them in their jobs.

Business people can use them in selling and in presentations. Teachers can use them in communicating a concept (or to wake up a class that's dozing off). Some ministers and youth workers find illusions to be a marvelous means for teaching spiritual truths.

Parents and grandparents have discovered that sharing tricks with their children is a wonderful way to break down any communication barriers that might exist. "How'd you do that? Do it again!" your kids will say.

The Internet provides a great tool for learning illusions and card tricks, and most are absolutely free. A fabulous link to vast resources of tricks is http://magic.miningco.com/msub10.htm.

Determine during this new millennial year to learn at least one new trick. Not only will it increase your visibility and self-confidence, it may help you in your business and strengthen family relationships.

THE NEXT STEP

A great book: *101 Amazing Card Tricks* by Bob Longe.

101 Things To Do In The Year 2000

MEMORIZE THE PREAMBLE TO THE CONSTITUTION

"We the people of the United States, in order to form a more perfect union, establish justice, insure domestic tranquillity, provide for the common defense, promote the general welfare, and secure the blessings of liberty to ourselves . . ."

—Preamble to the Constitution of the United States

96

The years have taken their toll and most Americans, including myself, have forgotten the words. But as the new millennium begins, we need to read it again and rethink the ramifications and blessings of this one sentence. It speaks so eloquently and precisely of the freedoms we have as Americans.

In order to appreciate the Preamble in a different way, talk to immigrants who have escaped harsh conditions in their native countries to come here. Try to go to court when they are being sworn in as new citizens, and listen to them recite the Pledge of Allegiance to the American flag. Ask them about the "blessings of liberty."

As a result of the early colonists' vision, dedication, and shed blood, we live today in a land of justice, peace, security, blessings, and liberty. Resolve that during the year 2000 you will relearn, word for word, the Preamble to the Constitution of the United States.

THE NEXT STEP

The full text of the Constitution can be read on the Web site at www.usconstitution.net/const.html.

ASSEMBLE A JIGSAW PUZZLE WITH YOUR LOVED ONES

"The tragedy of life doesn't lie in not reaching your goal. The tragedy lies in having no goal to reach."

—Benjamin E. Mays

97

One Christmas when I was about ten years old, I received a jigsaw puzzle as a gift. It had more pieces than I had ever seen. For a youngster to put together a puzzle with a thousand pieces, it is somewhat daunting. I still remember the picture on that puzzle—the gorgeous snowcapped mountains and the reflection of their majestic beauty in a crystalline lake. This reflection, of course, made it doubly hard to find the correct pieces as I worked on it.

My mother pulled the old folding card table from the closet, and that became my work place. Many evenings (this was before we owned a television), my sister, mother, and dad joined me to work on that puzzle. Those were some of the most memorable times we had together as a family.

Today's families have little quality time together, and working a puzzle may be just as enjoyable for your family as it was for mine. If you have children, you can take them with you to select the puzzle, and order pizza or make popcorn for a treat as you start the puzzle session. Decide on a time when everyone can be present, and begin the puzzle on a surface where it can remain until it is finished. A large puzzle will probably take a number of sessions to assemble, and some nights you may have to tear the family away from it.

THE NEXT STEP

Celebrate a winter's evening in the year 2000 by assembling a jigsaw puzzle with your family. You'll enjoy both the relaxed fun and the concentration of the evening.

DONATE BLOOD
TO THE LOCAL BLOOD BANK

"Do not wait for leaders. Do it alone, person to person."

—Mother Teresa

98

Christy White would never have lived without donated blood. It saved her life. All told, she needed forty-eight pints. Increasingly, people like Christy are needing blood after accidents, during surgery, or to supplement some deficiency in their own system.

The nation's blood supply is becoming more critical, and the need for blood donors is growing. One of the biggest concerns is that the most faithful blood donors are those who lived through World War II, and that group is getting smaller and smaller. They have now entered the age group of those who need more blood, but those of younger generations aren't donating blood to meet the growing needs. Some major cities across the United States are now importing blood from other regions and from overseas just to meet the need.

Each day in the United States, only 40,000 people donate blood, and many of them are donating their own blood for their later use in nonemergency surgery. If this number of donors continues to decrease and the need for blood among the over-fifty age group continues to increase, the nation's blood supply will be facing a crisis sometime in the early 2000s.

THE NEXT STEP

If you're currently donating blood, you are to be commended. But if you're not a donor and you're healthy, resolve now to give the gift of life in the new millennium by donating blood to your local blood bank.

LEARN THE ART
OF GIVING A MASSAGE

"No act of kindness, no matter how small, is ever wasted."

—Aesop

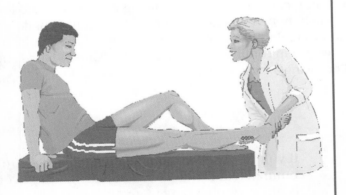

99

Wouldn't a massage feel great right now? Those were my thoughts as I was walking through the airport in Providence, Rhode Island, recently. I saw something that I'd never seen before—a mechanical massage machine. What a great idea after a long trip. All a person had to do was insert a few dollars, sit down in the massage chair, and for fifteen minutes or so the machine would do the rest. Because I was running late, I had to pass, but next time I know where I'm headed to get a massage.

What benefits can you give with a massage?

- One of the foremost benefits is relaxation. It's a great stress reliever and has the capacity to lessen the effects of fatigue.
- It relieves tightness and sore muscles.
- It improves circulation and loosens stiff, painful joints.
- It serves as a means of helping people put current problems into perspective.
- For married couples, one great benefit is the bonding that comes from physical touch.

Courses in massage therapy are available in many communities. Check your library or bookstore for one of the numerous books on learning the art of giving massage therapy.

THE NEXT STEP

Learn the art of giving a massage during the year 2000. Your spouse and family will be glad that you did.

GO A COMPLETE DAY
WITHOUT BECOMING ANGRY

"A hothead stirs up a fight, but one who holds his temper calms disputes."

—Proverbs 15:18 GOD'S WORD

100

Anger has become so much a part of life that some people can't imagine life without it. Road rage and office temper tantrums have become common occurrences.

What's your anger frequency rate? What really makes you explode? Check the following situations and take your anger temperature.

- Could you go a whole day without becoming angry even when the boss jumps on you or a coworker snaps at you for no reason at all?

- Could you keep your temper if you couldn't find your car keys or your checkbook?

- Could you avoid getting angry and soon forget it when some "stupid" driver cuts you off?

There's no doubt that people will continue to be angry, and some with good reason. Anger is here to stay, but where does it come from? Normally it's the result of hurt pride or unreasonable expectations. We use anger as a means of blaming others for our shortcomings, to boost our own egos, and to retaliate when we think someone has hurt us. It's our reaction to frustration or injury. But beware! As someone has said, anger is just one letter short of danger.

FINAL THOUGHT

 As you enter the year 2000, commit yourself to one anger-free day in which you won't lose your temper or get upset with somebody, something, or some situation. One day could lead to many.

SAY A PRAYER FOR THE LEADERS OF THE NATION

"I encourage you to make petitions, prayers, intercessions, and prayers of thanks for all people, for rulers, and for everyone who has authority over us. Pray for these people so that we can have a quiet and peaceful life."

—1 Timothy 2:1–2 GOD'S WORD

Billy Graham received some strong criticism after he prayed at the 1993 inauguration of President Clinton. Dr. Graham defended himself by saying, "I'm praying for the President, not for the party or platform. We're told to pray for people in authority."

The final two years of the twentieth century have been chaotic and tumultuous. American citizens, as never before, need to uphold our leaders in prayer—no matter what their party affiliation.

- First, pray for your governor and your state legislators.
- Next, pray for your members of Congress.
- Then, uphold the justices of the Supreme Court in your prayers.
- Finally, pray for the President and the President's family.

Your prayers should ask God:

- that the leaders of the country will be given wisdom and have firm convictions of right and wrong when judgments must be made.
- that they will not allow polls, lobbyists, news reporters, fame, pride, or any promise of financial gain to take precedence over what is right and best for the nation.

FINAL THOUGHT

Even if you ignore most of the other suggestions for the year 2000, don't skip this one. Commit yourself firmly to praying for the leaders of our country during this millennial year.

RESOURCE INDEX

1. Books: *All About Trees*—Ortho Books and *1001 Questions Answered About Trees*—Platt.
2. Information on fasting: *www.fasting.com/journaltoc.html*.
3. *Creating Keepsakes Scrapbook Magazine* at 888-247-5282. Helpful information: *http://www.scrapbooksupplies.com*.
4. Book: *Celebration of Discipline*—Richard J. Foster. Information: *http://www.aboutliving.com*.
5. Flip Album information: *http://www.ebooksys.com*.
6. Internet college education information: *http://www.geteducated.com*.
7. Good Internet sites: *http://www.americasbestonline.com* and *http://www.topclick.com*.
8. Telephone information: *http://www.555-1212.com* and *http://www.theultimates.com/white*.
9. Travel sites: *http://expedia.msn.com* and *http://city.net*.
10. Book: *The Complete Cookie: Cookies for Every Occasion*—Bluestein & Turner.
11. Alexis de Tocqueville at: *http://xroads.virginia.edu/*.
12. Time capsule call: Future Packaging & Preservation at 800-786-6627 or Time Capsules, Inc. at 800-527-7853.
13. This Web site offers excellent letter writing software: http://*writeexpress.com*.
14. Books: *The Life You've Always Wanted*—John Ortberg and *Experiencing God*—Blackaby & King.
15. Family Tree software: *www.familytreemaker.com*.
16. Internet public library: *http://www.ipl.org* and *http://www.elibrary.com*.
17. Books: *Journaling for Joy*—Joyce Chapman and *Journaling: A Spirit Journey*—Anne Broyles.
18. Tips for writing letters to representatives and senators: *http://www.cfll.org/tips.htm*.
19. *Quick Cooking* magazine: *www.reinmanpub.com*.
20. Parents letter: *http://ivansplace.com/a_parents_letter.htm*.
21. Great health site: *http://www.phys.com/a_home/01home/home.htm*.
22. Carnegie course information: *http://www.dalecarnegie.com*.
23. Book: *http://www.amazon.com* travel section for travel books on a specific state.
24. Book: *A Taste for Love: A Romantic Cookbook for Two*—Harbison & McGowan.
25. The book that inspired the movie, *Shadowlands: A Grief Observed*—C. S. Lewis.
26. Book: *Organizing from the Inside Out*—Julie Morgenstern.
    Free Internet personal organizer: *http://www.poww.com/poww/index.htm*.

27. Check the yellow pages for a local photographer.
28. Fabulous site for museums, zoos, and much more: *http://www.encyberpedia.com/eindex.htm*.
29. Portions of entry taken from: Lowell Streiker, *An Encyclopedia of Humor* (Peabody, MA: Hendrickson Publishers, 1998), 364.
   More clean jokes: *http://storypalace.ourfamily.com/index.html*.
30. The Bird House store: *http://www.tbh.com*.
31. Portions of entry taken from: H. Allen Smith, cited by Robert C. Shannon, *1000 Windows* (Cincinnati: Standard Publishing Co., 1977), and included in the *Bible Illustrator* 3.0, (Hiawatha, IA: Parson's Technology, 1999), CD-ROM.
   Book: *Art of Forgiving: When You Need to Forgive and Don't Know How*—Lewis Smedes.
32. Book that includes helpful software: *The Millionaire Kit: Surprisingly Simple Strategies for Building Real Wealth*—Nelson.
33. Book: *The Best Ice Cream Maker Cookbook Ever*—Peggy Fallon, John Boswell.
34. Portions of entry taken from: *Seattle Times* (January 5, 1999), 7A.
35. One of the best money information sites: *http://www.quicken.com*.
36. A link to major book clubs: *http://publishing.miningco.com/msub25.htm?terms=book+clubs&COB=home*.
37. Online discount store for skates: *http://www.skatemall.com* or call toll-free 877-597-1734.
38. Habitat for Humanity Web site: *http://www.habitat.org*.
39. Check out Dining à la Card where you receive 20% rebates: *http://www.dalc.com*.
40. Web site for foreign language information: *http://www.call.gov/index/htm*.
41. Book: *He's Gonna Toot and I'm Gonna Scoot*—Barbara Johnson.
42. Portions of entry taken from: Sharon Hodge, "Whose Birthday Is This, Anyway?" *Minneapolis Star Tribune* (December 25, 1997), 16A, as quoted on Electric Library at *www.elibrary.com*.
   Book: *In the Fullness of Time: A Historian Looks at Christmas, Easter, and the Early Church*—Paul L. Maier.
43. Great resource site for the gardener: *http://gardening.miningco.com/mbody.htm*.
44. Learn new words: *http://www.m-w.com*.
45. Book: *Discover What You're Best At* Linda Gale.
46. Book: *The Platinum Rule*—Alessandra & O'Connor.
47. Book: *Simplify Your Household*—Aronson (part of the wonderful Simpler Life series).
48. Good site for financial resources: *http://www.pathfinder.com/money/plus/index.oft*.
49. Books: *Elements of Style*—Strunk and White and *Bird by Bird*—Anne Lamott.
50. Portions of entry taken from: Alan Caruba, "The Plague of Boredom," *The World & I*, vol. 13 (January 1, 1998), 318, as quoted on Electric Library at *www.elibrary.com*.
   Good site for hobbies: *http://home.miningco.com/hobbies*.

51. Information on darts: *http://www.osgoods.com/link.html*.
52. Books: *Organize Your Home* and *Organize Your Office*—both by Eisenberg & Kelly.
53. Goodwill Industries Web site: *http://www.goodwill.org*.
54. Performing arts information site: *http://home.miningco.com/arts/perfarts*.
55. Web site link for ordering flowers: *http://www.4flowers.com*.
56. Book resource: *http://www.acses.com*.
57. Arthur Murray Web site: *http://www.dancetonight.com*.
58. Portions of entry taken from: "The Balloonists' Prayer," as quoted on the Shasta Valley Balloons page at *www.hot-airballoons.com*.
    Hot-air balloon information: *http://www.launch.net/* and *http://www.hot-airballoons.com/*.
59. Web sites on charities: *http://www.guidestar.org* and *http://www.give.org*.
60. Book: *Basket of Blessings: 31 Days to a More Grateful Heart*—Karen O'Connor.
61. Send e-mail greeting cards: *http://marlo.com/birthday.htm* and *http://www.egreetings.com*.
62. Book (an overview of Ecclesiastes): *Soul Search*—Ricker and Pitkin.
63. Fodor's B&B Web site: *http://travel.epicurious.com/travel/b_places/05_bnb/intro.html*.
64. The Water Works information: *http://capestorm.com/water.htm*.
65. Book: *What's So Amazing About Grace?*—Philip Yancy
66. Book: *E-Mail for Dummies*—Levine (ed.). Free e-mail at: *http://hotmail.com*.
67. Book: *The Giving Tree*—Shel Silverstein.
68. Another Internet source for news: *http://www.worldnetdaily.com*.
69. Discover the top 10 oceans and lakes: *http://www.planet101.com/geography.htm*.
70. Quiz game: *The Bible Brain Quest*—Dan Penwell.
71. Parks: *www.americanparks.com/locator.htm* and *http://usparks.miningco.com/mbody.htm*.
72. Portions of entry taken from: Charles A. Kroloff, *54 Ways You Can Help the Homeless* (New York: Hugh Lauter Levin Assoc., 1993), 11–13.
    Web site for Volunteers of America: *http//www.voa.org*.
73. Shop for the best prices on a camera or camcorder: *http://www.bodo.com/shopping.htm*.
74. Book: *How to Win Friends and Influence People*—Dale Carnegie.
75. Portions of entry taken from: Lowell Streiker, *An Encyclopedia of Humor* (Peabody, MA: Publishers, 1998), 172–175.
    Book: *The Complete Idiot's Guide to Breaking Bad Habits*—Levert, McCalin, et al.
76. Organ donor information: *http://organdonor.gov/*.
77. Epitaphs on the Internet: *http://www.netins.net/showcase/kadinger/anthology.htm*.
78. Midisoft piano information: *http://www.provantage.com/scripts/go.dll/-s/fp_29634*.
79. Consider sending an e-mail thank you note: *http://www2.bluemountain.com/index.html*.
80. Portions of entry taken from: Rick Chillot, "What Are You Afraid Of? 8 Secrets That Make Fear Disappear," *Prevention*, vol. 50 (May 1, 1998), 98–104, as quoted on Electric Library at *www.elibrary.com*.

Book: *Overcoming Fear and Discouragement*—Kay Arthur, Bob Vereen & David Lawson.

81. Information on prisoners from prisoners: *http://www.cyberspace-inmates.com.*

82. Need meal or cooking information: *http://cookbooks.miningco.com/mlibrary.htm.*

83. Papa John's Pizza is growing fast: *http://www.papajohns.com.*

84. Brea, CA, is famous for block parties: *http://207.238.115.68/brea/blockparty/info.html.*

85. Book: *365 Romantic Gifts for Your Love: A Daily Guide to Creative Giving*—Tomima Edmark.

86. Richard Estrada, "Divorce and Nonmarriage Hurt Kids," *The Dallas Morning News* (August 23, 1996) as quoted on Electric Library at *www.elibrary.com.*
    Use the Internet to send animated, musical cards: *http://marlo.com.*

87. Entertainment Book can be contacted at 800-374-4464.

88. Book: *The Complete Idiot's Guide to Buying Insurance and Annuities*—Brian H. Breuel.

89. Check out the WillMaker 7.0 software at: *http://www.nolo.com.*

90. Search here for an out-of-print book: *http://www.bookfinder.com.*

91. Portions of entry taken from: *Houston Post* (January 2, 1995): 4C, quoted in Raymond McHenry, *Something to Think About* (Peabody, MA: Hendrickson Publishers, 1998), 248-249.

92. Books: *10k and 5k Running, Training and Racing*—David Holt and *The Complete Idiot's Guide to Jogging and Running*—Rodgers and Douglas.

93. Books: *http://ww.amazon.com* and enter "1001" under title and find over 400 books filled with 1001 ideas each.

94. Plan your trip with a map: *http://www.mapsonus.com.*

95. Book: *101 Amazing Card Tricks*—Bob Longe.

96. Learn about the U.S. Constitution: *http://www.ourconstitution.com.*

97. Try a mystery and puzzle combination: *The Curse of the Mummy; Story and Jigsaw Puzzle Set with Book.*

98. Peg Meier, "In a Helpful Vein—The Nation's Blood Supply Is Under Strain," *Minneapolis Star Tribune* (January 31, 1999).
    Information from the American Assoc. of Blood Banks: *http://www.aabb.org.*

99. Book: *Massage for Beginners: The Eye-Level and Hands-Free Guide to the Art of Self and Partner Massage*—Marilyn Aslani.

100. An Internet tool kit for anger: *http://www.angermgmt.com/angertoolkit.html.*

101. Portions of entry taken from: Billy Graham, "1993 Inaugural Prayer," *Houston Chronicle* (January 23, 1993): 2E, as quoted by Raymond McHenry, *Something to Think About* (Peabody, MA: Hendrickson Publishers, 1998), 191-192.
    Book: *Prayer: Finding the Heart's True Home*—Richard Foster.

ABOUT THE AUTHOR

Dan Penwell, M. Div., is the best-selling author of the *Bible Brain Quest, The Tiny Bible,* and *Tiny Bible Promises.* He has been in Christian publishing for over 25 years with Family Christian Stores, World Bible Publishing, and is currently the manager of Trade Products at Hendrickson Publishers.

Dan was creator and producer of the complete line of audio Bible cassettes and CDs for both World and Hendrickson. At Family Christian stores, he was instrumental in recognizing and developing Frank Peretti and Max Lucado into national, best-selling authors. Dan is also an ordained minister and an active Bible teacher. He lives in Haverhill, Massachusetts, with his wife, Gloria. They have three sons and a daughter—the two oldest sons being ordained ministers.

ENCYCLICAL LETTER

REDEMPTORIS MISSIO

OF THE SUPREME PONTIFF

JOHN PAUL II

ON THE

PERMANENT VALIDITY

OF THE

CHURCH'S MISSIONARY MANDATE

CONTENTS

CHAPTER IV
THE VAST HORIZONS
OF THE MISSION *AD GENTES*

CHAPTER V
THE PATHS OF MISSION

CHAPTER VI
LEADERS AND WORKERS
IN THE MISSIONARY APOSTOLATE

CHAPTER VII

COOPERATION IN MISSIONARY ACTIVITY

CHAPTER VIII

MISSIONARY SPIRITUALITY

JOHN PAUL PP. II

Venerable Brothers,
Beloved Sons and Daughters,
Health and the Apostolic Blessing!

INTRODUCTION

1. THE MISSION OF CHRIST the Redeemer, which is entrusted to the Church, is still very far from completion. As the second Millennium after Christ's coming draws to an end, an overall view of the human race shows that this mission is still only beginning and that we must commit ourselves wholeheartedly to its service. It is the Spirit who impels us to proclaim the great works of God: "For if I preach the Gospel, that gives me no ground for boasting. For necessity is laid upon me. Woe to me if I do not preach the Gospel!" (*1 Cor* 9:16).

In the name of the whole Church, I sense an urgent duty to repeat this cry of Saint Paul. From the beginning of my Pontificate I have chosen to travel to the ends of the earth in order to show this missionary concern. My direct contact with peoples who do not know Christ has convinced me even more of the *urgency of missionary activity,* a subject to which I am devoting the present Encyclical.

The Second Vatican Council sought to renew the Church's life and activity in the light of the needs of the contemporary world. The Council emphasized the Church's "missionary nature", basing it in a dynamic way on the Trinitarian mission itself. The missionary thrust therefore belongs to the very nature of the Christian life, and is also the inspiration behind ecumenism: "that they may all be one ... so that the world may believe that you have sent me" (*Jn* 17:21).

2. The Council has already borne much fruit in the realm of missionary activity. There has been an increase of local Churches with their own Bishops, clergy and workers in the apostolate. The presence of Christian communities is more evident in the life of nations, and communion between the Churches has led to a lively exchange of spiritual benefits and gifts. The commitment of the laity to the work of evangelization is changing ecclesial life, while particular Churches are more willing to meet with the members of other Christian Churches and other religions, and to enter into dialogue and cooperation with them. Above all, there is a new awareness that *missionary activity is a matter for all Christians,* for all dioceses and parishes, Church institutions and associations.

Nevertheless, in this "new springtime" of

Christianity there is an undeniable negative tendency, and the present Document is meant to help overcome it. Missionary activity specifically directed "to the nations" (*ad gentes*) appears to be waning, and this tendency is certainly not in line with the directives of the Council and of subsequent statements of the Magisterium. Difficulties both internal and external have weakened the Church's missionary thrust towards non- Christians, a fact which must arouse concern among all who believe in Christ. For in the Church's history, missionary drive has always been a sign of vitality, just as its lessening is a sign of a crisis of faith.[1]

Twenty-five years after the conclusion of the Council and the publication of the Decree on Missionary Activity *Ad Gentes*, fifteen years after the Apostolic Exhortation *Evangelii Nuntiandi* issued by Pope Paul VI, and in continuity with the magisterial teaching of my predecessors,[2] I wish to invite the Church to *renew her missionary commitment*. The present Document has as its goal an interior renewal

---

[1] Cf. PAUL VI, *Message* for World Mission Day, 1972, *Insegnamenti* X, (1972), 522: "How many internal tensions, which weaken and divide certain local Churches and institutions, would disappear before the firm conviction that the salvation of local communities is procured through cooperation in work for the spread of the Gospel to the farthest bounds of the earth!"

[2] Cf. BENEDICT XV, Apostolic Letter *Maximum Illud* (30 November 1919): *AAS* 11 (1919), 440-455; PIUS XI, Encyclical Letter *Rerum Ecclesiae* (28 February 1926): *AAS* 18 (1926), 65-83; PIUS XII, Encyclical Letter *Evangelii Praecones* (2 June 1951): *AAS* 43 (1951), 497-528; Encyclical Letter *Fidei Donum* (21 April 1957): *AAS* 49 (1957), 225-248; JOHN XXIII, Encyclical Letter *Princeps Pastorum* (28 November 1959): *AAS* 51 (1959), 833-864.

of faith and Christian life. For missionary activity renews the Church, revitalizes faith and Christian identity, and offers fresh enthusiasm and new incentive. *Faith is strengthened when it is given to others!* It is in commitment to the Church's universal mission that the new evangelization of Christian peoples will find inspiration and support.

But what moves me even more strongly to proclaim the urgency of missionary evangelization is the fact that it is the primary service which the Church can render to every individual and to all humanity in the modern world, a world which has experienced marvellous achievements but which seems to have lost its sense of ultimate realities and of existence itself. "Christ the Redeemer", I wrote in my first Encyclical, "fully reveals man to himself ... The man who wishes to understand himself thoroughly ... must ... draw near to Christ ... The] Redemption that took place through the Cross has definitively restored to man his dignity and given back meaning to his life in the world"[3].

I also have other reasons and aims: to respond to the many requests for a document of this kind; to clear up doubts and ambiguities regarding missionary activity *ad gentes*, and to confirm in their commitment those exemplary brothers and sisters dedicated to missionary

[3] Encyclical Letter *Redemptor Hominis* (4 March 1979), 10: *AAS* 71 (1979), 274f.

6

activity and all those who assist them; to foster missionary vocations; to encourage theologians to explore and expound systematically the various aspects of missionary activity; to give a fresh impulse to missionary activity by fostering the commitment of the particular Churches—especially those of recent origin—to send forth and receive missionaries; and to assure non-Christians and particularly the authorities of countries to which missionary activity is being directed that all of this has but one purpose: to serve man by revealing to him the love of God made manifest in Jesus Christ.

3. *Peoples everywhere, open the doors to Christ!* His Gospel in no way detracts from man's freedom, from the respect that is owed to every culture and to whatever is good in each religion. By accepting Christ, you open yourselves to the definitive Word of God, to the One in whom God has made himself fully known and has shown us the path to himself.

The number of those who do not know Christ and do not belong to the Church is constantly on the increase. Indeed, since the end of the Council it has almost doubled. When we consider this immense portion of humanity which is loved by the Father and for whom he sent his Son, the urgency of the Church's mission is obvious.

On the other hand, our own times offer the Church new opportunities in this field: we have witnessed the collapse of oppressive ideologies and political systems; the opening of frontiers and the formation of a more united world due to an increase in communications; the affirmation among peoples of the Gospel values which Jesus made incarnate in his own life (peace, justice, brotherhood, concern for the needy); and a kind of soulless economic and technical development which only stimulates the search for the truth about God, about man and about the meaning of life itself.

God is opening before the Church the horizons of a humanity more fully prepared for the sowing of the Gospel. I sense that the moment has come to commit all of the Church's energies to a new evangelization and to the mission *ad gentes*. No believer in Christ, no institution of the Church can avoid this supreme duty: to proclaim Christ to all peoples.

Chapter I

JESUS CHRIST, THE ONLY SAVIOUR

4. In my first Encyclical, in which I set forth the programme of my Pontificate, I said that "the Church's fundamental function in every age, and particularly in ours, is to direct man's gaze, to point the awareness and experience of the whole of humanity towards the mystery of Christ".[4]

The Church's universal mission is born of faith in Jesus Christ, as is stated in our Trinitarian profession of faith: "I believe in one Lord, Jesus Christ, the only Son of God, eternally begotten of the Father ... For us men and for our salvation he came down from heaven: by the power of the Holy Spirit he became incarnate from the Virgin Mary, and was made man".[5] The Redemption event brings salvation to all, "for each one is included in the mystery of the Redemption and with each one Christ has united himself for ever through this mystery".[6] It is only in faith that the

[4] *Ibid.: loc. cit.*, 275.
[5] Nicene-Constantinopolitan Creed: *DS* 150.
[6] Encyclical Letter *Redemptor Hominis*, 13: *loc. cit.*, 283.

9

Church's mission can be understood and only in faith that it find its basis.

Nevertheless, also as a result of the changes which have taken place in modern times and the spread of new theological ideas, some people wonder: *"Is missionary work among non-Christians still relevant? Has it not been replaced by inter-religious dialogue? Is not human development an adequate goal of the Church's mission? Does not respect for conscience and for freedom exclude all efforts at conversion? Is it not possible to attain salvation in any religion? Why then should there be missionary activity?*

"No one comes to the Father, but by me" (*Jn* 14:6)

5. If we go back to the beginnings of the Church, we find a clear affirmation that Christ is the one Saviour of all, the only one able to reveal God and lead to God. In reply to the Jewish religious authorities who question the Apostles about the healing of the lame man, Peter says: "By the name of Jesus Christ of Nazareth whom you crucified, whom God raised from the dead, by him this man is standing before you well ... And there is salvation in no one else, for there is no other name under heaven given among men by which we must be saved" (*Acts* 4:10, 12). This statement, which was made to the Sanhedrin, has a uni-

versal value, since for all people—Jews and Gentiles alike—salvation can only come from Jesus Christ.

The universality of this salvation in Christ is asserted throughout the New Testament. Saint Paul acknowledges the Risen Christ as the Lord. He writes: "Although there may be so-called gods in heaven or on earth—as indeed there are many 'gods' and many 'lords'—yet for us there is one God, the Father, from whom are all things and for whom we exist, and one Lord, Jesus Christ, through whom are all things and through whom we exist" (1 *Cor* 8:5-6). One God and one Lord are asserted by way of contrast to the multitude of "gods" and "lords" commonly accepted. Paul reacts against the polytheism of the religious environment of his time and emphasizes what is characteristic of the Christian faith: belief in one God and in one Lord sent by God.

In the Gospel of Saint John, this salvific universality of Christ embraces all the aspects of his mission of grace, truth and revelation: the Word is "the true light that enlightens every man" (*Jn* 1:9). And again, "no one has ever seen God; the only Son, who is in the bosom of the Father, he has made him known" (*Jn* 1:18; cf. *Mt* 11:27). God's revelation becomes definitive and complete through his only-begotten Son: "In many and various ways God spoke of old to our fathers by the prophets; but in these last days he has spoken to us by a Son, whom he appointed the heir of all things, through whom he also created the world" (*Heb* 1:1-2; cf. *Jn* 14:6). In this definitive Word of his revelation, God has made himself known in the fullest possible way. He has revealed to mankind *who he is*. This definitive self-revelation of God is the fundamental reason why the Church is missionary by her very nature. She cannot do other than proclaim the Gospel, that is, the fullness of the truth which God has enabled us to know about himself.

Christ is the one mediator between God and mankind: "For there is one God, and there is one mediator between God and men, the man Christ Jesus, who gave himself as a ransom for all, the testimony to which was borne at the proper time. For this I was appointed a preacher and apostle (I am telling the truth, I am not lying), a teacher of the Gentiles in faith and truth" (*1 Tim* 2:5-7; cf. *Heb* 4:14-16). No one, therefore, can enter into communion with God except through Christ, by the working of the Holy Spirit. Christ's one, universal mediation, far from being an obstacle on the journey towards God, is the way established by God himself, a fact of which Christ is fully aware. Although participated forms of mediation of different kinds and degrees are not excluded, they acquire meaning and value *only* from Christ's own mediation, and they cannot be understood as parallel or complementary to his.

6. To introduce any sort of separation between the Word and Jesus Christ is contrary to the Christian faith. Saint John clearly states that the Word, who "was in the beginning with God", is the very one who "became flesh" (*Jn* 1:2, 14). Jesus is the Incarnate Word—a single and indivisible person. One cannot separate Jesus from the Christ or speak of a "Jesus of history" who would differ from the "Christ of faith". The Church acknowledges and confesses Jesus as "the Christ, the Son of the living God" (*Mt* 16:16): Christ is none other than Jesus of Nazareth; he is the Word of God made man for the salvation of all. In Christ "the whole fullness of deity dwells bodily" (*Col* 2:9) and "from his fulness have we all received" (*Jn* 1:16). The "only Son, who is in the bosom of the Father" (*Jn* 1:18) is "the beloved Son, in whom we have redemption ... For in him all the fulness of God was pleased to dwell, and through him to reconcile to himself all things, whether on earth or in heaven, making peace by the blood of his Cross" (*Col* 1:13-14, 19-20). It is precisely this uniqueness of Christ which gives him an absolute and universal significance, whereby, while belonging to history, he remains history's centre and goal:[7] "I am the Alpha and the Omega, the first

---

[7] Cf. SECOND VATICAN ECUMENICAL COUNCIL, Pastoral Constitution on the Church in the World of Today *Gaudium et Spes*, 2.

and the last, the beginning and the end" (*Rev* 22:13).

Thus, although it is legitimate and helpful to consider the various aspects of the mystery of Christ, we must never lose sight of its unity. In the process of discovering and appreciating the manifold gifts–especially the spiritual treasures–that God has bestowed on every people, we cannot separate those gifts from Jesus Christ, who is at the centre of God's plan of salvation. Just as "by his incarnation the Son of God united himself in some sense with every human being", so too "we are obliged to hold that the Holy Spirit offers everyone the possibility of sharing in the Paschal Mystery in a manner known to God".[8] God's plan is "to unite all things in Christ, things in heaven and things on earth" (*Eph* 1:10).

FAITH IN CHRIST
IS DIRECTED TO MAN'S FREEDOM

7. The urgency of missionary activity derives from the *radical newness of life* brought by Christ and lived by his followers. This new life is a gift from God, and people are asked to accept and develop it, if they wish to realize the fulness of their vocation in conformity to Christ. The whole New Testament is a hymn to the new life of those who believe in Christ and live in his Church. Salvation in Christ, as

[8] *Ibid.,* 22.

14

witnessed to and proclaimed by the Church, is God's self-communication: "It is love which not only creates the good, but also grants participation in the very life of God: Father, Son and Holy Spirit. For he who loves desires to give himself".[9]

God offers mankind this newness of life. "Can one reject Christ and everything that he has brought about in the history of mankind? Of course one can. Man is free. He can say 'no' to God. He can say 'no' to Christ. But the fundamental question remains: Is it legitimate to do this? And what would make it legitimate?"[10]

8. In the modern world there is a tendency to reduce man to his horizontal dimension alone. But without an openness to the Absolute, what does man become? The answer to this question is found in the experience of every individual, but it is also written in the history of humanity with the blood shed in the name of ideologies or by political regimes which have sought to build a "new humanity" without God.[11]

Moreover, the Second Vatican Council replies to those concerned with safeguarding freedom of conscience: "the human person has

[9] Encyclical Letter *Dives in Misericordia* (30 November 1980), 7: *AAS* 72 (1980), 1202.

[10] *Homily* for the celebration of the Eucharist in Krakow, 10 June 1979: *AAS* 71 (1979), 873.

[11] Cf. JOHN XXIII, Encyclical Letter *Mater et Magistra* (15 May 1961), IV: *AAS* 53 (1961), 451-453.

a right to religious freedom... all should have such immunity from coercion by individuals, or by groups, or by any human power, that no one should be forced to act against his conscience in religious matters, nor prevented from acting according to his conscience, whether in private or in public, whether alone or in association with others, within due limits".[12]

Proclaiming Christ and bearing witness to him, when done in a way that respects consciences, does not violate freedom. Faith demands a free adherence on the part of man, but at the same time faith must also be offered to him, because the "multitudes have the right to know the riches of the mystery of Christ—riches in which we believe that the whole of humanity can find, in unsuspected fulness, everything that it is gropingly searching for concerning God, man and his destiny, life and death, and truth. ... This is why the Church keeps her missionary spirit alive, and even wishes to intensify it in the moment of history in which we are living".[13] But it must also be stated, again with the Council, that "in accordance with their dignity as persons, equipped with reason and free will and endowed with personal responsibility, all are impelled by their own nature and are bound by a moral obligation to seek truth, above all religious truth.

---

[12] Declaration on Religious Freedom *Dignitatis Humanae,* 2.

[13] PAUL VI, Apostolic Exhortation *Evangelii Nuntiandi* (8 December 1975), 53: *AAS* 68 (1976), 42.

16

They are further bound to hold to the truth once it is known, and to regulate their whole lives by its demands".[14]

THE CHURCH AS SIGN
AND INSTRUMENT OF SALVATION

9.   The first beneficiary of salvation is the Church. Christ won the Church for himself at the price of his own blood and made the Church his co-worker in the salvation of the world. Indeed, Christ dwells within the Church. She is his Bride. It is he who causes her to grow. He carries out his mission through her.

The Council makes frequent reference to the Church's role in the salvation of mankind. While acknowledging that God loves all people and grants them the possibility of being saved (cf. *1 Tim* 2:4),[15] the Church believes that God has established Christ as the one mediator and that she herself has been established as the universal sacrament of salvation.[16] "To this catholic unity of the people of God, therefore, ... all are called, and they belong to it or are ordered to it in various ways,

---

[14] Declaration on Religious Freedom *Dignitatis Humanae*, 2.

[15] Cf. Dogmatic Constitution on the Church *Lumen Gentium*, 14-17; Decree on the Missionary Activity of the Church *Ad Gentes*, 3.

[16] Cf. Dogmatic Constitution on the Church *Lumen Gentium*, 48; Pastoral Constitution on the Church in the World of Today *Gaudium et Spes*, 43; Decree on the Missionary Activity of the Church *Ad Gentes*, 7, 21.

whether they be Catholic faithful or others who believe in Christ or finally all people everywhere who by the grace of God are called to salvation".[17] It is necessary to keep these two truths together, namely, the real possibility of salvation in Christ for all mankind and the necessity of the Church for salvation. Both these truths help us to understand the *one mystery of salvation,* so that we can come to know God's mercy and our own responsibility. Salvation, which always remains a gift of the Spirit, requires man's cooperation, both to save himself and to save others. This is God's will, and this is why he established the Church and made her a part of his plan of salvation. Referring to "this messianic people", the Council says: "It has been set up by Christ as a communion of life, love and truth; by him too it is taken up as the instrument of salvation for all, and sent on a mission to the whole world as the light of the world and the salt of the earth".[18]

SALVATION IN CHRIST IS OFFERED TO ALL

10. The universality of salvation means that it is granted not only to those who explicitly believe in Christ and have entered the Church. Since salvation is offered to all, it

[17] Dogmatic Constitution on the Church *Lumen Gentium,* 13.
[18] *Ibid.,* 9.

18

must be made concretely available to all. But it is clear that today, as in the past, many people do not have an opportunity to come to know or accept the Gospel revelation or to enter the Church. The social and cultural conditions in which they live do not permit this, and frequently they have been brought up in other religious traditions. For such people salvation in Christ is accessible by virtue of a grace which, while having a mysterious relationship to the Church, does not make them formally part of the Church but enlightens them in a way which is accommodated to their spiritual and material situation. This grace comes from Christ; it is the result of his Sacrifice and is communicated by the Holy Spirit. It enables each person to attain salvation through his or her free cooperation.

For this reason the Council, after affirming the centrality of the Paschal Mystery, went on to declare that "this applies not only to Christians but to all people of good will in whose hearts grace is secretly at work. Since Christ died for everyone, and since the ultimate calling of each of us comes from God and is therefore a universal one, we are obliged to hold that the Holy Spirit offers everyone the possibility of sharing in this Paschal Mystery in a manner known to God".[19]

[19] Pastoral Constitution on the Church in the World of Today *Gaudium et Spes*, 22.

11. What then should be said of the objections already mentioned regarding the mission *ad gentes?* While respecting the beliefs and sensitivities of all, we must first clearly affirm our faith in Christ, the one Saviour of mankind, a faith we have received as a gift from on high, not as a result of any merit of our own. We say with Paul, "I am not ashamed of the Gospel: it is the power of God for salvation to every one who has faith" (*Rom* 1:16). Christian martyrs of all times–including our own–have given and continue to give their lives in order to bear witness to this faith, in the conviction that every human being needs Jesus Christ, who has conquered sin and death and reconciled mankind to God.

Confirming his words by miracles and by his Resurrection from the dead, Christ proclaimed himself to be the Son of God dwelling in intimate union with the Father, and was recognized as such by his disciples. The Church offers mankind the Gospel, that prophetic message which responds to the needs and aspirations of the human heart and always remains "Good News". The Church cannot fail to proclaim that Jesus came to reveal the face of God and to merit salvation for all mankind by his Cross and Resurrection.

To the question, *"why mission?"*, we reply with the Church's faith and experience that true liberation consists in opening oneself to the love of Christ. In him, and only in him, are we set free from all alienation and doubt, from slavery to the power of sin and death. Christ is truly "our peace" (*Eph* 2:14); "the love of Christ impels us" (*2 Cor* 5:14), giving meaning and joy to our life. *Mission is an issue of faith,* an accurate indicator of our faith in Christ and his love for us.

The temptation today is to reduce Christianity to merely human wisdom, a pseudo-science of well-being. In our heavily secularized world a "gradual secularization of salvation" has taken place, so that people strive for the good of man, but man who is truncated, reduced to his merely horizontal dimension. We know, however, that Jesus came to bring integral salvation, one which embraces the whole person and all mankind, and opens up the wondrous prospect of divine filiation. *Why mission?* Because to us, as to Saint Paul, "this grace was given, to preach to the Gentiles the unsearchable riches of Christ" (*Eph* 3:8). Newness of life in him is the "Good News" for men and women of every age: all are called to it and destined for it. Indeed, all people are searching for it, albeit at times in a confused way, and have a right to know the value of this gift and to approach it freely. The Church, and every individual Christian within her, may not keep hidden or monopolize this newness and richness which has been received from God's bounty in order to be communicated to all mankind.

This is why the Church's mission derives not only from the Lord's mandate but also from the profound demands of God's life within us. Those who are incorporated in the Catholic Church ought to sense their privilege and for that very reason their greater obligation of *bearing witness to the faith and to the Christian life* as a service to their brothers and sisters and as a fitting response to God. They should be ever mindful that "they owe their distinguished status not to their own merits but to Christ's special grace; and if they fail to respond to this grace in thought, word and deed, not only will they not be saved, they will be judged more severely".[20]

---

[20] SECOND VATICAN ECUMENICAL COUNCIL, Dogmatic Constitution on the Church *Lumen Gentium*, 14.

CHAPTER II

THE KINGDOM OF GOD

12.   "It is 'God, who is rich in mercy' whom Jesus Christ has revealed to us as Father: it is his very Son who, in himself, has manifested him and made him known to us".[21] I wrote this at the beginning of my Encyclical *Dives in Misericordia,* to show that Christ is the revelation and incarnation of the Father's mercy. Salvation consists in believing and accepting the mystery of the Father and of his love, made manifest and freely given in Jesus through the Spirit. In this way the Kingdom of God comes to be fulfilled: the Kingdom prepared for in the Old Testament, brought about by Christ and in Christ, and proclaimed to all peoples by the Church, which works and prays for its perfect and definitive realization.

The Old Testament attests that God chose and formed a people for himself, in order to reveal and carry out his loving plan. But at the same time God is the Creator and Father of all people; he cares and provides for them, extending his blessing to all (cf. Gen 12:3); he

---

[21] Encyclical Letter *Dives in Misericordia,* 1: *loc. cit.,* 1177.

has established a covenant with all of them (cf. *Gen* 9:1-17). Israel experiences a personal and saving God (cf. *Dt* 4:37; 7:6-8; *Is* 43:1-7) and becomes his witness and interpreter among the nations. In the course of her history, Israel comes to realize that her election has a universal meaning (cf. for example *Is* 2:2-5; 25:6-8; 60:1-6; *Jer* 3:17; 16:19).

CHRIST MAKES THE KINGDOM PRESENT

13.   Jesus of Nazareth brings God's plan to fulfilment. After receiving the Holy Spirit at his Baptism, Jesus makes clear his messianic calling: he goes about Galilee "preaching the Gospel of God and saying: 'The time is fulfilled, and the Kingdom of God is at hand; repent and believe in the Gospel' " (*Mk* 1:14-15; cf. *Mt* 4:17; *Lk* 4:43). The proclamation and establishment of God's Kingdom are the purpose of his mission: "I was sent for this purpose" (*Lk* 4:43). But that is not all. Jesus himself is the "Good News", as he declares at the very beginning of his mission in the synagogue at Nazareth, when he applies to himself the words of Isaiah about the Anointed One sent by the Spirit of the Lord (cf. *Lk* 4:14-21). Since the "Good News" is Christ, there is an identity between the message and the messenger, between saying, doing and being. His power, the secret of the effectiveness of his actions, lies in his total identification with the message he announces: he proclaims the "Good

News" not just by what he says or does, but by what he is.

The ministry of Jesus is described in the context of his journeys within his homeland. Before Easter, the scope of his mission was focused on Israel. Nevertheless, Jesus offers a new element of extreme importance. The eschatological reality is not relegated to a remote "end of the world", but is already close and at work in our midst. The Kingdom of God is at hand (cf. *Mk* 1:15); its coming is to be prayed for (cf. *Mt* 6:10); faith can glimpse it already at work in signs such as miracles (cf. *Mt* 11:4-5) and exorcisms (cf. *Mt* 12:25-28), in the choosing of the Twelve (cf. *Mk* 3:13-19), and in the proclamation of the Good News to the poor (cf. *Lk* 4:18). Jesus' encounters with Gentiles make it clear that entry into the Kingdom comes through faith and conversion (cf. *Mk* 1:15), and not merely by reason of ethnic background.

The Kingdom which Jesus inaugurates is the Kingdom of God. Jesus himself reveals who this God is, the One whom he addresses by the intimate term "Abba", Father (cf. *Mk* 14:36). God, as revealed above all in the parables (cf. *Lk* 15:3-32; *Mt* 20:1-16), is sensitive to the needs and sufferings of every human being: he is a Father filled with love and compassion, who grants forgiveness and freely bestows the favours asked of him.

Saint John tells us that "God is love" (*1 Jn* 4:8, 16). Every person therefore is invited to "repent" and to "believe" in God's merciful love. The Kingdom will grow insofar as every person learns to turn to God in the intimacy of prayer as to a Father (cf. *Lk* 11:2; *Mt* 23:9) and strives to do his will (cf. *Mt* 7:21).

CHARACTERISTICS OF THE KINGDOM AND ITS DEMANDS

14.   Jesus gradually reveals the characteristics and demands of the Kingdom through his words, his actions and his own person.

The Kingdom of God is meant for all mankind, and all people are called to become members of it. To emphasize this fact, Jesus drew especially near to those on the margins of society, and showed them special favour in announcing the Good News. At the beginning of his ministry he proclaimed that he was "anointed ... to preach good news to the poor" (*Lk* 4:18). To all who are victims of rejection and contempt Jesus declares: "Blessed are you poor" (*Lk* 6:20). What is more, he enables such individuals to experience liberation even now, by being close to them, going to eat in their homes (cf. *Lk* 5:30; 15:2), treating them as equals and friends (cf. *Lk* 7:34), and making them feel loved by God, thus revealing his tender care for the needy and for sinners (cf. *Lk* 15:1-32).

The liberation and salvation brought by the Kingdom of God come to the human person both in his physical and spiritual dimensions. Two gestures are characteristic of Jesus' mission: healing and forgiving. Jesus' many healings clearly show his great compassion in the face of human distress, but they also signify that in the Kingdom there will no longer be sickness or suffering, and that his mission, from the very beginning, is meant to free people from these evils. In Jesus' eyes, healings are also a sign of spiritual salvation, namely liberation from sin. By performing acts of healing, he invites people to faith, conversion and the desire for forgiveness (cf. *Lk* 5:24). Once there is faith, healing is an encouragement to go further: it leads to salvation (cf. *Lk* 18:42-43). The acts of liberation from demonic possession—that supreme evil and symbol of sin and rebellion against God—are signs that indeed "the Kingdom of God has come upon you" (*Mt* 12:28).

15. The Kingdom aims at transforming human relationships; it grows gradually as people slowly learn to love, forgive and serve one another. Jesus sums up the whole Law, focusing it on the commandment of love (cf. *Mt* 22:34-40; *Lk* 10:25-28). Before leaving his disciples, he gives them a "new commandment": "Love one another; even as I have loved you" (*Jn* 13:34; cf. 15:12). Jesus' love for the world finds its highest expression in the gift of his life for mankind (cf. *Jn* 15:13), which manifests the love which the Father has for the world (cf. *Jn*

3:16). The Kingdom's nature, therefore, is one of communion among all human beings—with one another and with God.

The Kingdom is the concern of everyone: individuals, society, and the world. Working for the Kingdom means acknowledging and promoting God's activity, which is present in human history and transforms it. Building the Kingdom means working for liberation from evil in all its forms. In a word, the Kingdom of God is the manifestation and the realization of God's plan of salvation in all its fulness.

IN THE RISEN CHRIST GOD'S KINGDOM IS FULFILLED AND PROCLAIMED

16. By raising Jesus from the dead, God has conquered death, and in Jesus he has definitively inaugurated his Kingdom. During his earthly life, Jesus was the Prophet of the Kingdom; after his Passion, Resurrection and Ascension into heaven he shares in God's power and in his dominion over the world (cf. *Mt* 28:18; *Acts* 2:36; *Eph* 1:18-21). The Resurrection gives a universal scope to Christ's message, his actions and whole mission. The disciples recognize that the Kingdom is already present in the person of Jesus and is slowly being established within man and the world through a mysterious connection with him.

Indeed, after the Resurrection, the disciples preach the Kingdom by proclaiming Jesus Crucified and Risen from the dead. In Samaria,

Philip "preached good news about the Kingdom of God and the name of Jesus Christ" (*Acts* 8:12). In Rome, we find Paul "preaching the Kingdom of God and teaching about the Lord Jesus Christ" (*Acts* 28:31). The first Christians also proclaim "the Kingdom of Christ and of God" (*Eph* 5:5; cf. *Rev* 11:15; 12:10), or "the Kingdom of our Lord and Saviour Jesus Christ" (*2 Pt* 1:11). The preaching of the early Church was centred on the proclamation of Jesus Christ, with whom the Kingdom was identified. Now, as then, there is a need to unite *the proclamation of the Kingdom of God* (the content of Jesus' own "kerygma") and *the proclamation of the Christ-event* (the "kerygma" of the Apostles). The two proclamations are complementary; each throws light on the other.

THE KINGDOM IN RELATION TO CHRIST AND THE CHURCH

17.   Nowadays the Kingdom is much spoken of, but not always in a way consonant with the thinking of the Church. In fact, there are ideas about salvation and mission which can be called "anthropocentric" in the reductive sense of the word, inasmuch as they are focused on man's earthly needs. In this view, the Kingdom tends to become something completely human and secularized; what counts are programmes and struggles for a liberation which is socio-economic, political and even cultural,

but within a horizon that is closed to the transcendent. Without denying that on this level too there are values to be promoted, such a notion nevertheless remains within the confines of a kingdom of man, deprived of its authentic and profound dimensions. Such a view easily translates into one more ideology of purely earthly progress. The Kingdom of God, however, "is not of this world ... is not from the world" (Jn 18:36).

There are also conceptions which deliberately emphasize the Kingdom and which describe themselves as "Kingdom-centred". They stress the image of a Church which is not concerned about herself, but which is totally concerned with bearing witness to and serving the Kingdom. It is a "Church for others" just as Christ is the "man for others". The Church's task is described as though it had to proceed in two directions: on the one hand promoting such "values of the Kingdom" as peace, justice, freedom, brotherhood, etc., while on the other hand fostering dialogue between peoples, cultures and religions, so that through a mutual enrichment they might help the world to be renewed and to journey ever closer towards the Kingdom.

Together with positive aspects, these conceptions often reveal negative aspects as well. First, they are silent about Christ: the Kingdom . of which they speak is "theocentrically" based, since, according to them, Christ cannot be understood by those who lack Christian

30

faith, whereas different peoples, cultures and religions are capable of finding common ground in the one divine reality, by whatever name it is called. For the same reason they put great stress on the mystery of creation, which is reflected in the diversity of cultures and beliefs, but they keep silent about the mystery of redemption. Furthermore, the Kingdom, as they understand it, ends up either leaving very little room for the Church or undervaluing the Church in reaction to a presumed "ecclesiocentrism" of the past, and because they consider the Church herself only a sign, for that matter a sign not without ambiguity.

18.   This is not the Kingdom of God as we know it from Revelation. The Kingdom cannot be detached either from Christ or from the Church.

As has already been said, Christ not only proclaimed the Kingdom, but in him the Kingdom itself became present and was fulfilled. This happened not only through his words and his deeds: "Above all, . . . the Kingdom is made manifest in the very person of Christ, Son of God and Son of Man, who came 'to serve and to give his life as a ransom for many' (*Mk* 10:45)".[22] The Kingdom of God is not a concept, a doctrine, or a programme subject to free interpretation, but is before all

---

[22] SECOND VATICAN ECUMENICAL COUNCIL, Dogmatic Constitution on the Church *Lumen Gentium*, 5.

else *a person* with the face and name of Jesus of Nazareth, the image of the invisible God.[23] If the Kingdom is separated from Jesus, it is no longer the Kingdom of God which he revealed. The result is a distortion of the meaning of the Kingdom, which runs the risk of being transformed into a purely human or ideological goal, and a distortion of the identity of Christ, who no longer appears as the Lord to whom everything must one day be subjected (cf. *1 Cor* 15:27).

Likewise, one may not separate the Kingdom from the Church. It is true that the Church is not an end unto herself, since she is ordered towards the Kingdom of God of which she is the seed, sign and instrument. Yet, while remaining distinct from Christ and the Kingdom, the Church is indissolubly united to both. Christ endowed the Church, his Body, with the fulness of the benefits and means of salvation. The Holy Spirit dwells in her, enlivens her with his gifts and charisms, sanctifies, guides and constantly renews her.[24] The result is a unique and special relationship which, while not excluding the action of Christ and the Spirit outside the Church's visible boundaries, confers upon her a specific and necessary role; hence the Church's special

[23] Cf. SECOND VATICAN ECUMENICAL COUNCIL, Pastoral Constitution on the Church in the World of Today *Gaudium et Spes,* 22.

[24] Cf. SECOND VATICAN ECUMENICAL COUNCIL, Dogmatic Constitution on the Church *Lumen Gentium,* 4.

connection with the Kingdom of God and of Christ, which she has "the mission of announcing and inaugurating among all peoples".[25]

19. It is within this overall perspective that the reality of the Kingdom is understood. Certainly, the Kingdom demands the promotion of human values, as well as those which can properly be called "evangelical", since they are intimately bound up with the "Good News". But this sort of promotion, which is at the heart of the Church, must not be detached from or opposed to other fundamental tasks, such as proclaiming Christ and his Gospel, and establishing and building up communities which make present and active within mankind the living image of the Kingdom. One need not fear falling thereby into a form of "ecclesiocentrism". Pope Paul VI, who affirmed the existence of "a profound link between Christ, the Church and evangelization",[26] also said that the Church "is not an end unto herself, but rather is fervently concerned to be completely of Christ, in Christ and for Christ, as well as completely of men, among men and for men".[27]

---

[25] *Ibid.,* 5.

[26] Apostolic Exhortation *Evangelii Nuntiandi,* 16: *loc. cit.,* 15.

[27] *Address* at the opening of the Third Session of the Second Vatican Ecumenical Council, 14 September 1964: *AAS* 56 (1964), 810.

The Church at the Service
of the Kingdom

20.   The Church is effectively and concretely at the service of the Kingdom. This is seen especially in her preaching, which is a call to conversion. Preaching constitutes the Church's first and fundamental way of serving the coming of the Kingdom in individuals and in human society. Eschatological salvation begins even now in newness of life in Christ: "To all who believed in him, who believed in his name, he gave power to become children of God" (*Jn* 1:12).

The Church, then, serves the Kingdom by establishing communities and founding new particular Churches, and by guiding them to mature faith and charity in openness towards others, in service to individuals and society, and in understanding and esteem for human institutions.

The Church serves the Kingdom by spreading throughout the world the "Gospel values" which are an expression of the Kingdom and which help people to accept God's plan. It is true that the inchoate reality of the Kingdom can also be found beyond the confines of the Church among peoples everywhere, to the extent that they live "Gospel values" and are open to the working of the Spirit who breathes when and where he wills (cf. *Jn* 3:8). But it must immediately be added that this temporal dimension of the Kingdom remains incomplete unless it is related to the Kingdom of Christ present in the Church and straining towards eschatological fulness.[28]

The many dimensions of the Kingdom of God [29] do not weaken the foundations and purposes of missionary activity, but rather strengthen and extend them. The Church is the sacrament of salvation for all mankind, and her activity is not limited only to those who accept her message. She is a dynamic force in mankind's journey towards the eschatological Kingdom, and is the sign and promoter of Gospel values.[30] The Church contributes to mankind's pilgrimage of conversion to God's plan through her witness and through such activities as dialogue, human promotion, commitment to justice and peace, education and the care of the sick, and aid to the poor and to children. In carrying on these activities, however, she never loses sight of the priority of the transcendent and spiritual realities which are premises of eschatological salvation.

Finally, the Church serves the Kingdom by her intercession, since the Kingdom by its very nature is God's gift and work, as we are

[28] Cf. PAUL VI, Apostolic Exhortation *Evangelii Nuntiandi*, 34: *loc. cit.,* 28.
[29] Cf. International Theological Commission, Select Themes of Ecclesiology on the Occasion of the Twentieth Anniversary of the Closing of the Second Vatican Council (7 October 1985), 10: "The Eschatological Character of the Church: Kingdom and Church".
[30] Cf. SECOND VATICAN ECUMENICAL COUNCIL, Pastoral Constitution on the Church in the World of Today *Gaudium et Spes,* 39.

reminded by the Gospel parables and by the prayer which Jesus taught us. We must ask for the Kingdom, welcome it and make it grow within us; but we must also work together so that it will be welcomed and will grow among all people, until the time when Christ "delivers the Kingdom to God the Father" and "God will be everything to every one" (cf. *1 Cor* 15:24, 28).

CHAPTER III

THE HOLY SPIRIT
THE PRINCIPAL AGENT OF MISSION

21. "At the climax of Jesus' messianic
mission, the Holy Spirit becomes present in the
Paschal Mystery in all of his divine subjec-
tivity: as the one who is now to continue the
salvific work rooted in the sacrifice of the
Cross. Of course Jesus entrusts this work to
human beings: to the Apostles, to the Church.
Nevertheless, in and through them the Holy
Spirit remains the transcendent and principal
agent for the accomplishment of this work in
the human spirit and in the history of the
world".[31]

The Holy Spirit is indeed the principal
agent of the whole of the Church's mission.
His action is preeminent in the mission *ad gentes,* as can clearly be seen in the early Church:
in the conversion of Cornelius (cf. *Acts* 10), in
the decisions made about emerging problems
(cf. *Acts* 15) and in the choice of regions and
peoples to be evangelized (cf. *Acts* 16:6 ff).
The Spirit worked through the Apostles, but

---

[31] Encyclical Letter *Dominum et Vivificantem* (18 May 1986), 42:
AAS 78 (1986), 857.

at the same time he was also at work in those who heard them: "Through his action the Good News takes shape in human minds and hearts and extends through history. In all of this it is the Holy Spirit who gives life".[32]

SENT FORTH
"TO THE END OF THE EARTH" (*Acts* 1:8)

22.   All the Evangelists, when they describe the Risen Christ's meeting with his Apostles, conclude with the "missionary mandate": "All authority in heaven and on earth has been given to me. Go therefore and make disciples of all nations, ... and lo, I am with you always, to the close of the age" (*Mt* 28:18-20; cf. *Mk* 16:15-18; *Lk* 24:46-49; *Jn* 20:21-23).

This is *a sending forth in the Spirit,* as is clearly apparent in the Gospel of John: Christ sends his own into the world, just as the Father has sent him, and to this end he gives them the Spirit. Luke, for his part, closely links the witness the Apostles are to give to Christ with the working of the Spirit, who will enable them to fulfil the mandate they have received.

23.   The different versions of the "missionary mandate" contain common elements as well as characteristics proper to each. Two elements, however, are found in all the versions. First,

---

[32] *Ibid.,* 64: *loc. cit.,* 892.

there is the universal dimension of the task entrusted to the Apostles, who are sent to "all nations" (*Mt* 28:19); "into all the world and ... to the whole creation" (*Mk* 16:15); to "all nations" (*Lk* 24:47); "to the end of the earth" (*Acts* 1:8). Secondly, there is the assurance given to the Apostles by the Lord that they will not be alone in this task, but will receive the strength and the means necessary to carry out their mission. The reference here is to the presence and power of the Spirit and the help of Jesus himself: "And they went forth and preached everywhere, while the Lord worked with them" (*Mk* 16:20).

As for the different emphases found in each version, Mark presents mission as proclamation or kerygma: "Preach the Gospel" (*Mk* 16:15). His aim is to lead his readers to repeat Peter's profession of faith: "You are the Christ" (*Mk* 8:29), and to say with the Roman centurion who stood before the body of Jesus on the Cross: "Truly this man was the Son of God!" (*Mk* 15:39). In Matthew, the missionary emphasis is placed on the foundation of the Church and on her teaching (cf. *Mt* 28:19-20; 16:18). According to him, the mandate shows that the proclamation of the Gospel must be completed by a specific ecclesial and sacramental catechesis. In Luke, mission is presented as witness (cf. *Lk* 24:48; *Acts* 1:8), centred especially on the Resurrection (cf. *Acts* 1:22). The missionary is invited to believe in the transforming power of the Gospel and to proclaim what Luke presents so well, that is, conversion to God's love and mercy, the experience of a complete liberation which goes to the root of all evil, namely sin.

John is the only Evangelist to speak explicitly of a "mandate", a word equivalent to "mission". He directly links the mission which Jesus entrusts to his disciples with the mission which he himself has received from the Father: "As the Father has sent me, even so I send you" (*Jn* 20:21). Addressing the Father, Jesus says: "As you sent me into the world, so I have sent them into the world" (*Jn* 17:18). The entire missionary sense of John's Gospel is expressed in the "priestly prayer": "This is eternal life, that they know you the only true God, and Jesus Christ whom you have sent" (*Jn* 17:3). The ultimate purpose of mission is to enable people to share in the communion which exists between the Father and the Son. The disciples are to live in unity with one another, remaining in the Father and the Son, so that the world may know and believe (cf. *Jn* 17:21-23). This is a very important missionary text. It makes us understand that we are missionaries above all because of *what we are* as a Church whose innermost life is unity in love, even before we become missionaries *in word or deed*.

The four Gospels therefore bear witness to a certain pluralism within the fundamental unity of the same mission, a pluralism which reflects different experiences and situations within the first Christian communities. It is also the result of the driving force of the Spirit himself; it encourages us to pay heed to the variety of missionary charisms and to the diversity of circumstances and peoples. Nevertheless, all the Evangelists stress that the mission of the disciples is to cooperate in the mission of Christ: "Lo, I am with you always, to the close of the age" (*Mt* 28:20). Mission, then, is based not on human abilities but on the power of the Risen Lord.

THE SPIRIT DIRECTS THE CHURCH'S MISSION

24.   The mission of the Church, like that of Jesus, is God's work or, as Luke often puts it, the work of the Spirit. After the Resurrection and Ascension of Jesus, the Apostles have a powerful experience which completely transforms them: the experience of Pentecost. The coming of the Holy Spirit makes them *witnesses* and *prophets* (cf. *Acts* 1:8; 2:17-18). It fills them with a serene courage which impels them to pass on to others their experience of Jesus and the hope which motivates them. The Spirit gives them the ability to bear witness to Jesus with "boldness".[33]

When the first evangelizers go down from Jerusalem, the Spirit becomes even more of a "guide", helping them to choose both those

[33] The Greek word "parrhesia" also means enthusiasm or energy; cf. *Acts* 2:29; 4:13, 29, 31; 9:27-28; 13:46; 14:3; 18:26; 19:8, 26; 28:31.

to whom they are to go and the places to which their missionary journey is to take them. The working of the Spirit is manifested particularly in the impetus given to the mission which, in accordance with Christ's words, spreads out from Jerusalem to all of Judea and Samaria, and to the farthest ends of the earth.

The Acts of the Apostles records six summaries of the "missionary discourses" which were addressed to the Jews during the Church's infancy (cf. *Acts* 2:22-39; 3:12-26; 4:9-12; 5:29-32; 10:34-43; 13:16-41). These model speeches, delivered by Peter and by Paul, proclaim Jesus and invite those listening to "be converted", that is, to accept Jesus in faith and to let themselves be transformed in him by the Spirit.

Paul and Barnabas are impelled by the Spirit to go to the Gentiles (cf. *Acts* 13:46-48), a development not without certain tensions and problems. How are these converted Gentiles to live their faith in Jesus? Are they bound by the traditions of Judaism and the law of circumcision? At the first Council, which gathers the members of the different Churches together with the Apostles in Jerusalem, a decision is taken which is acknowledged as coming from the Spirit: it is not necessary for a Gentile to submit to the Jewish Law in order to become a Christian (cf. *Acts* 15:5-11, 28). From now on the Church opens her doors and becomes the house which all may enter, and in which all can feel at home, while keeping their own culture and traditions, provided that these are not contrary to the Gospel.

25. The missionaries continued along this path, taking into account people's hopes and expectations, their anguish and sufferings, as well as their culture, in order to proclaim to them salvation in Christ. The speeches in Lystra and Athens (cf. *Acts* 14:15-17; 17:22-31) are acknowledged as models for the evangelization of the Gentiles. In these speeches Paul enters into "dialogue" with the cultural and religious values of different peoples. To the Lycaonians, who practised a cosmic religion, he speaks of religious experiences related to the cosmos. With the Greeks he discusses philosophy and quotes their own poets (cf. *Acts* 17:18, 26-28). The God whom Paul wishes to reveal is already present in their lives; indeed, this God has created them and mysteriously guides nations and history. But if they are to recognize the true God, they must abandon the false gods which they themselves have made and open themselves to the One whom God has sent to remedy their ignorance and satisfy the longings of their hearts. These are speeches which offer an example of the inculturation of the Gospel.

Under the impulse of the Spirit, the Christian faith is decisively opened to the "nations". Witness to Christ spreads to the most important centres of the eastern Mediterranean and then to Rome and the far regions of the West. It is the Spirit who is the source of the drive to press on, not only geographically but also beyond the frontiers of race and religion, for a truly universal mission.

The Holy Spirit
Makes the Whole Church Missionary

26.   The Spirit leads the company of believers to "form a community", to be the Church. After Peter's first proclamation on the day of Pentecost and the conversions that followed, the first community takes shape (cf. *Acts* 2:42-47; 4:32-35).

One of the central purposes of mission is to bring people together in hearing the Gospel, in fraternal communion, in prayer and in the Eucharist. To live in "fraternal communion" (*koinonia*) means to be "of one heart and soul" (*Acts* 4:32), establishing fellowship from every point of view: human, spiritual and material. Indeed, a true Christian community is also committed to distributing earthly goods, so that no one is in want, and all can receive such goods "as they need" (cf. *Acts* 2:45; 4:35). The first communities, made up of "glad and generous hearts" (*Acts* 2:46), were open and missionary: they enjoyed "favour with all the people" (*Acts* 2:47). Even before activity, mission means witness and a way of life that shines out to others.[34]

27.   The Acts of the Apostles indicates that the mission which was directed first to Israel and then to the Gentiles develops on many levels. First and foremost, there is the group of the Twelve which as a single body, led by Peter, proclaims the Good News. Then there is the community of believers, which in its way of life and its activity bears witness to the Lord and converts the Gentiles (cf. *Acts* 2:46-47). Then there are the special envoys sent out to proclaim the Gospel. Thus the Christian community at Antioch sends its members forth on mission; having fasted, prayed and celebrated the Eucharist, the community recognizes that the Spirit has chosen Paul and Barnabas to be "sent forth" (cf. *Acts* 13:1-4). In its origins, then, mission is seen as a community commitment, a responsibility of the local Church, which needs "missionaries" in order to push forward towards new frontiers. Side by side with those who had been sent forth, there were also others, who bore spontaneous witness to the newness which had transformed their lives, and who subsequently provided a link between the emerging communities and the Apostolic Church.

Reading the Acts of Apostles helps us to realize that at the beginning of the Church

---

[34] Cf. PAUL VI, Apostolic Exhortation *Evangelii Nuntiandi*, 41-42: *loc. cit.*, 31-33.

the mission *ad gentes*, while it had missionaries dedicated "for life" by a special vocation, was in fact considered the normal outcome of Christian living, to which every believer was committed through the witness of personal conduct and through explicit proclamation whenever possible.

THE SPIRIT IS PRESENT AND ACTIVE IN EVERY TIME AND PLACE

28.   The Spirit manifests himself in a special way in the Church and in her members. Nevertheless, his presence and activity are universal, limited neither by space nor time.[35] The Second Vatican Council recalls that the Spirit is at work in the heart of every person, through the "seeds of the Word", to be found in human initiatives—including religious ones—and in man's efforts to attain truth, goodness and God himself.[36]

The Spirit offers the human race "the light and strength to respond to its highest calling"; through the Spirit, "mankind attains in faith to the contemplation and savouring of the mystery of God's design"; indeed, "we are obliged to hold that the Holy Spirit offers

[35] Cf. Encyclical Letter *Dominum et Vivificantem*, 53: *loc. cit.*, 874f.
[36] Cf. SECOND VATICAN ECUMENICAL COUNCIL, Decree on the Missionary Activity of the Church *Ad Gentes*, 3, 11, 15; Pastoral Constitution on the Church in the World of Today *Gaudium et Spes*, 10-11, 22, 26, 38, 41, 92-93.

everyone the possibility of sharing in the Paschal Mystery in a manner known to God".[37] The Church "is aware that humanity is being continually stirred by the Spirit of God and can therefore never be completely indifferent to the problems of religion" and that "people will always ... want to know what meaning to give to their life, their activity and their death".[38] The Spirit, therefore, is at the very source of man's existential and religious questioning, a questioning which is occasioned not only by contingent situations but by the very structure of his being.[39]

The Spirit's presence and activity affect not only individuals but also society and history, peoples, cultures and religions. Indeed, the Spirit is at the origin of the noble ideals and undertakings which benefit humanity on its journey through history: "The Spirit of God with marvellous foresight directs the course of the ages and renews the face of the earth".[40] The Risen Christ "is now at work in human hearts through the strength of his Spirit, not only instilling a desire for the world to come but also thereby animating, purifying and reinforcing the noble aspirations which drive the human

---

[37] SECOND VATICAN ECUMENICAL COUNCIL, Pastoral Constitution on the Church in the World of Today *Gaudium et Spes*, 10, 15, 22.

[38] *Ibid.*, 41.

[39] Cf. Encyclical Letter *Dominum et Vivificantem*, 54: *loc. cit.*, 875f.

[40] SECOND VATICAN ECUMENICAL COUNCIL, Pastoral Constitution on the Church in the World of Today *Gaudium et Spes*, 26.

family to make its life one that is more human and to direct the whole earth to this end".[41] Again, it is the Spirit who sows the "seeds of the Word" present in various customs and cultures, preparing them for full maturity in Christ.[42]

29.   Thus the Spirit, who "blows where he wills" (cf. *Jn* 3:8), who "was already at work in the world before Christ was glorified"[43], and who "has filled the world, ... holds all things together (and) knows what is said" (*Wis* 1:7), leads us to broaden our vision in order to ponder his activity in every time and place.[44] I have repeatedly called this fact to mind, and it has guided me in my meetings with a wide variety of peoples. The Church's relationship with other religions is dictated by a twofold respect: "Respect for man in his quest for answers to the deepest questions of his life, and respect for the action of the Spirit in man".[45] Excluding any mistaken interpretation, the inter-religious meeting held in Assisi was meant to confirm

[41] *Ibid.,* 38; cf. 93.
[42] Cf. SECOND VATICAN ECUMENICAL COUNCIL, Dogmatic Constitution on the Church *Lumen Gentium,* 17; Decree on the Missionary Activity of the Church *Ad Gentes,* 3, 15.
[43] SECOND VATICAN ECUMENICAL COUNCIL, Decree on the Missionary Activity of the Church *Ad Gentes,* 4.
[44] Cf. Encyclical Letter *Dominum et Vivificantem,* 53: *loc. cit.,* 874.
[45] *Address* to Representatives of Non-Christian Religions, Madras, 5 February 1986: *AAS* 78 (1986), 767; cf. *Message to the Peoples of Asia,* Manila, 21 February 1981, 2-4: *AAS* 73 (1981), 392f; *Address* to Representatives of Other Religions, Tokyo, 24 February 1981, 3-4: *Insegnamenti* IV/I (1981), 507f.

my conviction that "every authentic prayer is prompted by the Holy Spirit, who is mysteriously present in every human heart".[46]

This is the same Spirit who was at work in the Incarnation and in the life, death and Resurrection of Jesus, and who is at work in the Church. He is therefore not an alternative to Christ, nor does he fill a sort of void which is sometimes suggested as existing between Christ and the Logos. Whatever the Spirit brings about in human hearts and in the history of peoples, in cultures and religions serves as a preparation for the Gospel [47] and can only be understood in reference to Christ, the Word who took flesh by the power of the Spirit "so that as perfectly human he would save all human beings and sum up all things".[48]

Moreover, the universal activity of the Spirit is not to be separated from his particular activity within the Body of Christ, which is the Church. Indeed, it is always the Spirit who is at work, both when he gives life to the Church and impels her to proclaim Christ, and when he implants and develops his gifts in all individuals and peoples, guiding the Church to discover these gifts, to foster them and receive them through dialogue. Every form of the

---

[46] *Address* to Cardinals and the Roman Curia, 22 December 1986, 11: *AAS* 79 (1987), 1089.

[47] Cf. SECOND VATICAN ECUMENICAL COUNCIL, Dogmatic Constitution on the Church *Lumen Gentium,* 16.

[48] SECOND VATICAN ECUMENICAL COUNCIL, Pastoral Constitution on the Church in the World of Today *Gaudium et Spes,* 45; cf. Encyclical Letter *Dominum et Vivificantem,* 54: *loc. cit.,* 876.

Spirit's presence is to be welcomed with respect and gratitude, but the discernment of this presence is the responsibility of the Church, to which Christ gave his Spirit in order to guide her into all the truth (cf. *Jn* 16:13).

MISSIONARY ACTIVITY IS ONLY BEGINNING

30.   Our own time, with humanity on the move and in continual search, demands *a resurgence of the Church's missionary activity.* The horizons and possibilities for mission are growing ever wider, and we Christians are called to an apostolic courage based upon trust in the Spirit. *He is the principal agent of mission!*

The history of humanity has known many major turning points which have encouraged missionary outreach, and the Church, guided by the Spirit, has always responded to them with generosity and farsightedness. Results have not been lacking. Not long ago we celebrated the millennium of the evangelization of Rus' and the Slav peoples, and we are now preparing to celebrate the five hundredth anniversary of the evangelization of the Americas. Similarly, there have been recent commemorations of the centenaries of the first missions in various countries of Asia, Africa and Oceania. Today the Church must face other challenges and push forward to new frontiers, both in the initial mission *ad gentes* and in the new evangelization of those peoples who have already heard Christ proclaimed. Today all Christians, the particular Churches and the universal Church, are called to have the same courage that inspired the missionaries of the past, and the same readiness to listen to the voice of the Spirit.

CHAPTER IV

THE VAST HORIZONS
OF THE MISSION *AD GENTES*

31.   The Lord Jesus sent his Apostles to every person, people and place on earth. In the Apostles the Church received a universal mission—one which knows no boundaries— which involves the communication of salvation in its integrity according to that fulness of life which Christ came to bring (cf. *Jn* 10:10). The Church was "sent by Christ to reveal and communicate the love of God to all people and nations".[49]

This mission is one and undivided, having one origin and one final purpose; but within it, there are different tasks and kinds of activity. First, there is the missionary activity which we call *mission ad gentes,* in reference to the opening words of the Council's Decree on this subject. This is one of the Church's fundamental activities: it is essential and never-ending. The Church, in fact, "cannot withdraw from her *permanent mission of bringing the Gospel* to the multitudes —the millions and millions of men and

[49] SECOND VATICAN ECUMENICAL COUNCIL, Decree on the Missionary Activity of the Church *Ad Gentes,* 10.

women—who as yet do not know Christ the Redeemer of humanity. In a specific way this is the missionary work which Jesus entrusted and still entrusts each day to his Church".[50]

A Complex and Ever Changing Religious Picture

32. Today we face a religious situation which is extremely varied and changing. Peoples are on the move; social and religious realities which were once clear and well-defined are today increasingly complex. We need only think of certain phenomena such as urbanization, mass migration, the flood of refugees, the de-christianization of countries with ancient Christian traditions, the increasing influence of the Gospel and its values in overwhelmingly non-Christian countries, and the proliferation of messianic cults and religious sects. Religious and social upheaval makes it difficult to apply in practice certain ecclesial distinctions and categories to which we have become accustomed. Even before the Council it was said that some Christian cities and countries had become "mission territories"; the situation has certainly not improved in the years since then.

On the other hand, missionary work has been very fruitful throughout the world, so

[50] Apostolic Exhortation *Christifideles Laici* (30 December 1988), 35: *AAS* 81 (1989), 457.

that there are now well-established Churches, sometimes so sound and mature that they are able to provide for the needs of their own communities and even send personnel to evangelize in other Churches and territories. This is in contrast to some traditionally Christian areas which are in need of re-evangelization. As a result, some are questioning whether it is still appropriate to speak of *specific missionary activity* or specifically "missionary" areas, or whether we should speak instead of a *single missionary situation,* with one single mission, the same everywhere. The difficulty of relating this complex and changing reality to the mandate of evangelization is apparent in the "language of mission". For example, there is a certain hesitation to use the terms "missions" and "missionaries", which are considered obsolete and as having negative historical connotations. People prefer to use instead the noun "mission" in the singular and the adjective "missionary" to describe all the Church's activities.

This uneasiness denotes a real change, one which has certain positive aspects. The so-called return or "repatriation" of the *missions* into the Church's mission, the insertion of *missiology* into *ecclesiology,* and the integration of both areas into the Trinitarian plan of salvation, have given a fresh impetus to missionary activity itself, which is not considered a marginal task for the Church but is situated at the centre of her life, as a fundamental commitment of the whole People of God. Nevertheless, care must be taken to avoid the risk of putting very different situations on the same level and of reducing, or even eliminating, the Church's mission and missionaries *ad gentes*. To say that the whole Church is missionary does not preclude the existence of a specific mission *ad gentes,* just as saying that all Catholics must be missionaries not only does not exclude, but actually requires that there be persons who have a specific vocation to be "life-long missionaries *ad gentes*".

Mission *ad gentes* Retains Its Value

33.   The fact that there is a diversity of activities *in the Church's one mission* is not intrinsic to that mission, but arises from the variety of circumstances in which that mission is carried out.[51] Looking at today's world from the viewpoint of evangelization, we can distinguish *three situations.*

First, there is the situation which the Church's missionary activity addresses: peoples, groups and socio-cultural contexts in which Christ and his Gospel are not known, or which lack Christian communities sufficiently mature to be able to incarnate the faith in their own environment and proclaim it to other groups. This is mission *ad gentes* in the proper sense of the term.[52]

---

[51] Cf. Second Vatican Ecumenical Council, Decree on the Missionary Activity of the Church *Ad Gentes*, 6.
[52] Cf. *ibid.*

Secondly, there are Christian communities with adequate and solid ecclesial structures. They are fervent in their faith and in Christian living. They bear witness to the Gospel in their surroundings and have a sense of commitment to the universal mission. In these communities the Church carries out her activity and pastoral care.

Thirdly, there is an intermediate situation, particularly in countries with ancient Christian roots, and occasionally in the younger Churches as well, where entire groups of the baptized have lost a living sense of the faith, or even no longer consider themselves members of the Church, and live a life far removed from Christ and his Gospel. In this case what is needed is a "new evangelization" or a "re-evangelization".

34.   Missionary activity proper, namely the mission *ad gentes,* is directed to "peoples or groups who do not yet believe in Christ", "who are far from Christ", in whom the Church "has not yet taken root" [53] and whose culture has not yet been influenced by the Gospel.[54] It is distinct from other ecclesial activities inasmuch as it is addressed to groups and settings which are non-Christian because the preaching of the Gospel and the presence of the Church are either absent or insufficient. It can thus be

[53] Cf. *ibid.,* 6, 23, 27.
[54] Cf. PAUL VI, Apostolic Exhortation *Evangelii Nuntiandi,* 18-20: *loc. cit.,* 17-19.

characterized as the work of proclaiming Christ and his Gospel, building up the local Church and promoting the values of the Kingdom. The specific nature of this mission *ad gentes* consists in its being addressed to "non-Christians". It is therefore necessary to ensure that this specifically "missionary work that Jesus entrusted and still entrusts each day to his Church" [55] does not become an indistinguishable part of the overall mission of the whole People of God and as a result become neglected or forgotten.

On the other hand, the boundaries between *pastoral care of the faithful, new evangelization* and *specific missionary activity* are not clearly definable, and it is unthinkable to create barriers between them or to put them into water-tight compartments. Nevertheless, there must be no lessening of the impetus to preach the Gospel and to establish new Churches among peoples or communities where they do not yet exist, for this is the first task of the Church, which has been sent forth to all peoples and to the very ends of the earth. Without the mission *ad gentes*, the Church's very missionary dimension would be deprived of its essential meaning and of the very activity that exemplifies it.

Also to be noted is the real and growing *interdependence* which exists between these various saving activities of the Church. Each

[55] Apostolic Exhortation *Christifideles Laici*, 35: *loc. cit.*, 457.

of them influences, stimulates and assists the others. The missionary thrust fosters exchanges between the Churches and directs them towards the larger world, with positive influences in every direction. The Churches in traditionally Christian countries, for example, involved as they are in the challenging task of new evangelization, are coming to understand more clearly that they cannot be missionaries to non-Christians in other countries and continents unless they are seriously concerned about the non-Christians at home. Hence missionary activity *ad intra* is a credible sign and a stimulus for missionary activity *ad extra,* and vice versa.

To All Peoples, in spite of Difficulties

35.   The mission *ad gentes* faces an enormous task, which is in no way disappearing. Indeed, both from the numerical standpoint of demographic increase and from the socio-cultural standpoint of the appearance of new relationships, contacts and changing situations, the mission seems destined to have ever wider horizons. The task of proclaiming Jesus Christ to all peoples appears to be immense and out of all proportion to the Church's human resources.

The difficulties seem insurmountable and could easily lead to discouragement, if it were a question of a merely human enterprise. In certain countries missionaries are refused entry. In others, not only is evangelization forbidden but conversion as well, and even Christian worship. Elsewhere the obstacles are of a cultural nature: passing on the Gospel message seems irrelevant or incomprehensible, and conversion is seen as a rejection of one's own people and culture.

36. Nor are *difficulties* lacking *within* the People of God; indeed these difficulties are the most painful of all. As the first of these difficulties Pope Paul VI pointed to "the lack of fervour (which) is all the more serious because it comes from within. It is manifested in fatigue, disenchantment, compromise, lack of interest and above all lack of joy and hope".[56] Other great obstacles to the Church's missionary work include past and present divisions among Christians,[57] de-christianization within Christian countries, the decrease of vocations to the apostolate, and the counter-witness of believers and Christian communities failing to follow the model of Christ in their lives. But one of the most serious reasons for the lack of interest in the missionary task is a widespread indifferentism, which, sad to say, is found also among Christians. It is based on incorrect theological perspectives and is characterised by a religious relativism which

---

[56] Apostolic Exhortation *Evangelii Nuntiandi*, 80: *loc. cit.*, 73.
[57] Cf. SECOND VATICAN ECUMENICAL COUNCIL, Decree on the Missionary Activity of the Church *Ad Gentes*, 6.

leads to the belief that "one religion is as good as another". We can add, using the words of Pope Paul VI, that there are also certain "excuses which would impede evangelization. The most insidious of these excuses are certainly the ones which people claim to find support for in such and such a teaching of the Council".[58]

In this regard, I earnestly ask theologians and professional Christian journalists to intensify the service they render to the Church's mission in order to discover the deep meaning of their work, along the sure path of "thinking with the Church" (*sentire cum Ecclesia*).

Internal and external difficulties must not make us pessimistic or inactive. What counts, here as in every area of Christian life, is the confidence that comes from faith, from the certainty that it is not we who are the principal agents of the Church's mission, but Jesus Christ and his Spirit. We are only co-workers, and when we have done all that we can, we must say: "We are unworthy servants; we have only done what was our duty" (*Lk* 17:10).

PARAMETERS OF THE CHURCH'S MISSION
AD GENTES

37.   By virtue of Christ's universal mandate, the mission *ad gentes* knows no boundaries.

---

[58] Apostolic Exhortation *Evangelii Nuntiandi*, 80: *loc. cit.*, 73.

Still, it is possible to determine certain parameters within which that mission is exercised, in order to gain a real grasp of the situation.

(a) *Territorial limits*. Missionary activity has normally been defined in terms of specific territories. The Second Vatican Council acknowledged the territorial dimension of the mission *ad gentes*,[59] a dimension which even today remains important for determining responsibilities, competencies and the geographical limits of missionary activity. Certainly, a universal mission implies a universal perspective. Indeed, the Church refuses to allow her missionary presence to be hindered by geographical boundaries or political barriers. But it is also true that missionary activity *ad gentes*, being different from the pastoral care of the faithful and the new evangelization of the non-practising, is exercised within well-defined territories and groups of people.

The growth in the number of new Churches in recent times should not deceive us. Within the territories entrusted to these Churches—particularly in Asia, but also in Africa, Latin America and Oceania—there remain vast regions still to be evangelized. In many nations entire peoples and cultural areas of great importance have not yet been reached

[59] Cf. Decree on the Missionary Activity of the Church *Ad Gentes*, 6.

by the proclamation of the Gospel and the presence of the local Church.[60] Even in traditionally Christian countries there are regions that are under the special structures of the mission *ad gentes,* with groups and areas not yet evangelized. Thus, in these countries too there is a need not only for a new evangelization, but also, in some cases, for an initial evangelization.[61]

Situations are not however the same everywhere. While acknowledging that statements about the missionary responsibility of the Church are not credible unless they are backed up by a serious commitment to a new evangelization in the traditionally Christian countries, it does not seem justified to regard as identical the situation of a people which has never known Jesus Christ and that of a people which has known him, accepted him and then rejected him, while continuing to live in a culture which in large part has absorbed Gospel principles and values. These are two basically different situations with regard to the faith.

Thus the criterion of geography, although somewhat imprecise and always provisional, is still a valid indicator of the frontiers towards which missionary activity must be directed. There are countries and geographical and

---

[60] Cf. *ibid.,* 20.
[61] Cf. *Address* to the members of the Symposium of the Council of the European Episcopal Conferences, 11 October 1985: *AAS* 78 (1986), 178-189.

cultural areas which lack indigenous Christian communities. In other places, these communities are so small as not to be a clear sign of a Christian presence; or they lack the dynamism to evangelize their societies, or belong to a minority population not integrated into the dominant culture of the nation. Particularly in Asia, towards which the Church's mission *ad gentes* ought to be chiefly directed, Christians are a small minority, even though sometimes there are significant numbers of converts and outstanding examples of Christian presence.

(b) *New worlds and new social phenomena.* The rapid and profound transformations which characterize today's world, especially in the southern hemisphere, are having a powerful effect on the overall missionary picture. Where before there were stable human and social situations, today everything is in flux. One thinks, for example, of urbanization and the massive growth of cities, especially where demographic pressure is greatest. In not a few countries, over half the population already lives in a few "megalopolises", where human problems are often aggravated by the feeling of anonymity experienced by masses of people.

In the modern age, missionary activity has been carried out especially in isolated regions which are far from centres of civilization and which are hard to penetrate because of difficulties of communication, language or climate. Today the image of mission *ad gentes* is perhaps changing: efforts should be concentrated on the big cities, where new customs and styles of living arise together with new forms of culture and communication, which then influence the wider population. It is true that the "option for the neediest" means that we should not overlook the most abandoned and isolated human groups, but it is also true that individuals or small groups cannot be evangelized if we neglect the centres where a new humanity, so to speak, is emerging, and where new models of development are taking shape. The future of the younger nations is being shaped in the cities.

Speaking of the future, we cannot forget the young, who in many countries comprise more than half the population. How do we bring the message of Christ to non-Christian young people who represent the future of entire continents. Clearly, the ordinary means of pastoral work are not sufficient: what are needed are associations, institutions, special centres and groups, and cultural and social initiatives for young people. This is a field where modern ecclesial movements have ample room for involvement.

Among the great changes taking place in the contemporary world, migration has produced a new phenomenon: non-Christians are becoming very numerous in traditionally Christian countries, creating fresh opportunities for contacts and cultural exchanges, and calling the Church to hospitality, dialogue, assistance and, in a word, fraternity. Among migrants, refugees occupy a very special place and deserve the greatest attention. Today, there are many millions of refugees in the world and their number is constantly increasing. They have fled from conditions of political oppression and inhuman misery, from famine and drought of catastrophic proportions. The Church must make them part of her overall apostolic concern.

Finally, we may mention the situations of poverty—often on an intolerable scale—which have been created in not a few countries, and which are often the cause of mass migration. The community of believers in Christ is challenged by these inhuman situations: the proclamation of Christ and the Kingdom of God must become the means for restoring the human dignity of these people.

(c) *Cultural sectors: the modern equivalents of the Areopagus*. After preaching in a number of places, Saint Paul arrived in Athens, where he went to the Areopagus and proclaimed the Gospel in language appropriate to and understandable in those surroundings (cf. *Acts* 17:22-31). At that time the Areopagus represented the cultural centre of the learned people of Athens, and today it can be taken as a symbol of the new sectors in which the Gospel must be proclaimed.

The first Areopagus of the modern age is the *world of communications*, which is unifying humanity and turning it into what is known as a "global village". The means of social communication have become so important as to be for many the chief means of information and education, of guidance and inspiration in their behaviour as individuals, families and within society at large. In particular, the younger generation is growing up in a world conditioned by the mass-media. To some degree perhaps this Areopagus has been neglected. Generally, preference has been given to other means of preaching the Gospel and of Christian education, while the mass-media are left to the initiative of individuals or small groups and enter into pastoral planning only in a secondary way. Involvement in the mass-media, however, is not meant merely to strengthen the preaching of the Gospel. There is a deeper reality involved here: since the very evangelization of modern culture depends to a great extent on the influence of the media, it is not enough to use the media simply to spread the Christian message and the Church's authentic teaching. It is also necessary to integrate that message into the "new culture" created by modern communications. This is a complex issue, since the "new culture" originates not just from whatever content is eventually expressed, but from the very fact that there exist new ways of communicating, with new languages, new techniques and a new psychology. Pope Paul VI said that "the split between the Gospel and culture is undoubtedly the tragedy of our time",[62] and the field of communications fully confirms this judgment.

There are many other forms of the "Areopagus" in the modern world towards which the Church's missionary activity ought to be directed; for example, commitment to peace, development and the liberation of peoples; the rights of individuals and peoples, especially those of minorities; the advancement of women and children; safeguarding the created world. These too are areas which need to be illuminated with the light of the Gospel.

We must also mention the immense "Areopagus" of culture, scientific research, and international relations which promote dialogue and open up new possibilities. We would do well to be attentive to these modern areas of activity and to be involved in them. People sense that they are as it were travelling together across life's sea, and that they are called to ever greater unity and solidarity. Solutions to pressing problems must be studied, discussed and worked out with the involvement of all. That is why international organizations and meetings are proving increasingly important in many sectors of human life, from culture to politics, from the economy to research. Christians who live and work in this international sphere must always

[62] Apostolic Exhortation *Evangelii Nuntiandi*, 20: *loc. cit.*, 19.

remember their duty to bear witness to the Gospel.

38.   Our times are both momentous and fascinating. While on the one hand people seem to be pursuing material prosperity and to be sinking ever deeper into consumerism and materialism, on the other hand we are witnessing a desperate search for meaning, the need for an inner life, and a desire to learn new forms and methods of meditation and prayer. Not only in cultures with strong religious elements, but also in secularized societies, the spiritual dimension of life is being sought after as an antidote to dehumanization. This phenomenon —the so-called "religious revival"—is not without ambiguity, but it also represents an opportunity. The Church has an immense spiritual patrimony to offer mankind, a heritage in Christ, who called himself "the way, and the truth, and the life" (*Jn* 14:6): it is the Christian path to meeting God, to prayer, to asceticism, and to the search for life's meaning. Here too there is an "Areopagus" to be evangelized.

FIDELITY TO CHRIST
AND THE PROMOTION OF HUMAN FREEDOM

39.   All forms of missionary activity are marked by an awareness that one is furthering human freedom by proclaiming Jesus Christ. The Church must be faithful to Christ, whose Body she is, and whose mission she continues.

68

She must necessarily "go the same road that Christ went—namely a road of poverty, obedience, service and self-sacrifice even unto death, from which he emerged a victor through his Resurrection".[63] The Church is thus obliged to do everything possible to carry out her mission in the world and to reach all peoples. And she has the right to do this, a right given her by God for the accomplishment of his plan. Religious freedom, which is still at times limited or restricted, remains the premise and guarantee of all the freedoms that ensure the common good of individuals and peoples. It is to be hoped that authentic religious freedom will be granted to all people everywhere. The Church strives for this in all countries, especially in those with a Catholic majority, where she has greater influence. But it is not a question of the religion of the majority or the minority, but of an inalienable right of each and every human person.

On her part, the Church addresses people with full respect for their freedom.[64] Her mission does not restrict freedom but rather promotes it. *The Church proposes; she imposes nothing.* She respects individuals and cultures,

[63] SECOND VATICAN ECUMENICAL COUNCIL, Decree on the Missionary Activity of the Church *Ad Gentes,* 5; cf. Dogmatic Constitution on the Church *Lumen Gentium,* 8.

[64] Cf. SECOND VATICAN ECUMENICAL COUNCIL, Declaration on Religious Freedom *Dignitatis Humanae,* 3-4; PAUL VI, Apostolic Exhortation *Evangelii Nuntiandi,* 79-80: *loc. cit.,* 71-75; JOHN PAUL II, Encyclical Letter *Redemptor Hominis,* 12: *loc. cit.,* 278-281.

and she honours the sanctuary of conscience. To those who for various reasons oppose missionary activity, the Church repeats: *Open the doors to Christ!*

Here I wish to address all the particular Churches, both young and old. The world is steadily growing more united, and the Gospel spirit must lead us to overcome cultural and nationalistic barriers, avoiding all isolationism. Pope Benedict XV already cautioned the missionaries of his time lest they "forget their proper dignity and think more of their earthly homeland than of their heavenly one".[65] This same advice is valid today for the particular Churches: Open the doors to missionaries, for "each individual Church that would voluntarily cut itself off from the universal Church would lose its relationship to God's plan and would be impoverished in its ecclesial mission".[66]

DIRECTING ATTENTION
TOWARDS THE SOUTH AND THE EAST

40. Today missionary activity still represents the greatest challenge for the Church. As the end of the second Millennium of the Redemption draws near, it is clear that the peoples which have not yet received an initial proclamation of Christ constitute the majority of mankind. The results of missionary activity

[65] Apostolic Letter *Maximum Illud: loc. cit.*, 446.
[66] PAUL VI, Apostolic Exhortation *Evangelii Nuntiandi*, 62: *loc. cit.*, 52.

in modern times are certainly positive. The Church has been established on every continent; indeed today the majority of believers and particular Churches is to be found no longer in Europe but on the continents which missionaries have opened up to the faith.

The fact remains however that the "ends of the earth" to which the Gospel must be brought are growing ever more distant. Tertullian's saying, that the Gospel has been proclaimed to all the earth and to all peoples,[67] is still very far from being a reality. The mission *ad gentes* is still in its infancy. New peoples appear on the world scene, and they too have a right to receive the proclamation of salvation. Population growth in non-Christian countries of the South and the East is constantly increasing the number of people who remain unaware of Christ's Redemption.

We need therefore to direct our attention towards those geographical areas and cultural settings which still remain uninfluenced by the Gospel. All who believe in Christ should feel, as an integral part of their faith, an apostolic concern to pass on to others its light and joy. This concern must become as it were a hunger and thirst to make the Lord known, given the vastness of the non-Christian world.

---

[67] Cf. *De praescriptione haereticorum*, XX: CCL I, 201f.

CHAPTER V

THE PATHS OF MISSION

41. "Missionary activity is nothing other and nothing less than the manifestation or epiphany of God's plan and its fulfilment in the world and in history; in this history God, by means of missions, clearly accomplishes the history of salvation".[68] What paths does the Church follow in order to achieve this goal?

Mission is a single but complex reality, and it develops in a variety of ways. Among these ways, some have particular importance in the present situation of the Church and the world.

THE FIRST FORM OF EVANGELIZATION IS WITNESS

42. People today put more trust in witnesses than in teachers,[69] in experience than in teaching, and in life and action than in theories. The witness of a Christian life is the first and irreplaceable form of mission: Christ, whose mission we continue, is the "witness" *par excellence* (*Rev* 1:5; 3:14) and the model of all Christian

---

[68] SECOND VATICAN ECUMENICAL COUNCIL, Decree on the Missionary Activity of the Church *Ad Gentes*, 9; cf. Chapter II, 10-18.

[69] Cf. PAUL VI, Apostolic Exhortation *Evangelii Nuntiandi*, 41: *loc. cit.*, 31f.

72

witness. The Holy Spirit accompanies the Church along her way and associates her with the witness he gives to Christ (cf. *Jn* 15:26-27).

The first form of witness is *the very life of the missionary, of the Christian family,* and *of the ecclesial community,* which reveal a new way of living. The missionary who, despite all his or her human limitations and defects, lives a simple life, taking Christ as the model, is a sign of God and of transcendent realities. But everyone in the Church, striving to imitate the Divine Master, can and must bear this kind of witness;[70] in many cases it is the only possible way of being a missionary.

The evangelical witness which the world finds most appealing is that of concern for people, and of charity towards the poor, the weak and those who suffer. The complete generosity underlying this attitude and these actions stands in marked contrast to human selfishness. It raises precise questions which lead to God and to the Gospel. A commitment to peace, justice, human rights and human promotion is also a witness to the Gospel when it is a sign of concern for persons and is directed towards integral human development.[71]

---

[70] Cf. SECOND VATICAN ECUMENICAL COUNCIL, Dogmatic Constitution on the Church *Lumen Gentium,* 28, 35, 38; Pastoral Constitution on the Church in the World of Today *Gaudium et Spes,* 43; Decree on the Missionary Activity of the Church *Ad Gentes,* 11-12.

[71] Cf. PAUL VI, Encyclical Letter *Populorum Progressio* (26 March 1967), 21, 42: *AAS* 59 (1967), 267f, 278.

43.   Christians and Christian communities are very much a part of the life of their respective nations and can be a sign of the Gospel in their fidelity to their native land, people and national culture, while always preserving the freedom brought by Christ. Christianity is open to universal brotherhood, for all men and women are sons and daughters of the same Father and brothers and sisters in Christ.

The Church is called to bear witness to Christ by taking courageous and prophetic stands in the face of the corruption of political or economic power; by not seeking her own glory and material wealth; by using her resources to serve the poorest of the poor and by imitating Christ's own simplicity of life. The Church and her missionaries must also bear the witness of humility, above all with regard to themselves—a humility which allows them to make a personal and communal examination of conscience in order to correct in their behaviour whatever is contrary to the Gospel and disfigures the face of Christ.

The Initial Proclamation of Christ the Saviour

44.   Proclamation is the permanent priority of mission. The Church cannot elude Christ's explicit mandate, nor deprive men and women of the "Good News" about their being loved and saved by God. "Evangelization will always contain—as the foundation, centre and at the

same time the summit of its dynamism—a clear proclamation that, in Jesus Christ ... salvation is offered to all men, as a gift of God's grace and mercy".[72] All forms of missionary activity are directed to this proclamation, which reveals and gives access to the mystery hidden for ages and made known in Christ (cf. *Eph* 3:3-9; *Col* 1:25-29), the mystery which lies at the heart of the Church's mission and life, as the hinge on which all evangelization turns.

In the complex reality of mission, initial proclamation has a central and irreplaceable role, since it introduces man "into the mystery of the love of God, who invites him to enter into a personal relationship with himself in Christ" [73] and opens the way to conversion. Faith is born of preaching, and every ecclesial community draws its origin and life from the personal response of each believer to that preaching.[74] Just as the whole economy of salvation has its centre in Christ, so too all missionary activity is directed to the proclamation of his mystery.

The subject of proclamation is Christ who was crucified, died and is risen: through him is accomplished our full and authentic liberation from evil, sin and death; through

[72] PAUL VI, Apostolic Exhortation *Evangelii Nuntiandi*, 27: *loc. cit.*, 23.
[73] SECOND - VATICAN ECUMENICAL COUNCIL, Decree on the Missionary Activity of the Church *Ad Gentes*, 13.
[74] Cf. PAUL VI, Apostolic Exhortation *Evangelii Nuntiandi*, 15: *loc. cit.*, 13-15; SECOND VATICAN ECUMENICAL COUNCIL, Decree on the Missionary Activity of the Church *Ad Gentes*, 13-14.

him God bestows "new life" that is divine and eternal. This is the "Good News" which changes man and his history, and which all peoples have a right to hear. This proclamation is to be made within the context of the lives of the individuals and peoples who receive it. It is to be made with an attitude of love and esteem towards those who hear it, in language which is practical and adapted to the situation. In this proclamation the Spirit is at work and establishes a communion between the missionary and his hearers, a communion which is possible inasmuch as both enter into communion with God the Father through Christ.[75]

45.   Proclamation, because it is made in union with the entire ecclesial community, is never a merely personal act. The missionary is present and carries out his work by virtue of a mandate he has received; even if he finds himself alone, he remains joined by invisible but profound bonds to the evangelizing activity of the whole Church.[76] Sooner or later, his hearers come to recognize in him the community which sent him and which supports him.

Proclamation is inspired by faith, which gives rise to enthusiasm and fervour in the

[75] Cf. Encyclical Letter *Dominum et Vivificantem,* 42, 64: *loc. cit.,* 857-859, 892-894.
[76] Cf. PAUL VI, Apostolic Exhortation *Evangelii Nuntiandi,* 60: *loc. cit.,* 50f.

missionary. As already mentioned, the Acts of the Apostles uses the word *parrhesia* to describe this attitude, a word which means to speak frankly and with courage. This term is found also in Saint Paul: "We had courage in our God to declare to you the Gospel of God in the face of great opposition" (*1 Th* 2:2); "Pray ... also for me, that utterance may be given me in opening my mouth boldly to proclaim the mystery of the Gospel for which I am an ambassador in chains; that I may declare it boldly, as I ought to speak" (*Eph* 6:18-20).

In proclaiming Christ to non-Christians, the missionary is convinced that, through the working of the Spirit, there already exists in individuals and peoples an expectation, even if an unconscious one, of knowing the truth about God, about man, and about how we are to be set free from sin and death. The missionary's enthusiasm in proclaiming Christ comes from the conviction that he is responding to that expectation, and so he does not become discouraged or cease his witness even when he is called to manifest his faith in an environment that is hostile or indifferent. He knows that the Spirit of the Father is speaking through him (cf. *Mt* 10:17-20; *Lk* 12:11-12) and he can say with the Apostles: "We are witnesses to these things, and so is the Holy Spirit" (*Acts* 5:32). He knows that he is not proclaiming a human truth, but the "word of God", which has an intrinsic and mysterious power of its own (cf. *Rom* 1:16).

The supreme test is the giving of one's life, to the point of accepting death in order to bear witness to one's faith in Jesus Christ. Throughout Christian history, martyrs, that is, "witnesses", have always been numerous and indispensable to the spread of the Gospel. In our own age, there are many: Bishops, priests, men and women Religious, lay people—often unknown heroes who give their lives to bear witness to the faith. They are *par excellence* the heralds and witnesses of the faith.

CONVERSION AND BAPTISM

46.   The proclamation of the word of God has *Christian conversion* as its aim: a complete and sincere adherence to Christ and his Gospel through faith. Conversion is a gift of God, a work of the Blessed Trinity. It is the Spirit who opens people's hearts so that they can believe in Christ and "confess him" (cf. *1 Cor* 12:3); of those who draw near to him through faith Jesus says: "No one can come to me unless the Father who sent me draws him" (*Jn* 6:44).

From the outset, conversion is expressed in faith which is total and radical, and which neither limits nor hinders God's gift. At the same time, it gives rise to a dynamic and life-long process which demands a continual turning away from "life according to the flesh" to "life according to the Spirit" (cf. *Rom* 8, 3-13). Conversion means accepting, by a personal decision, the saving sovereignty of Christ and becoming his disciple.

The Church calls all people to this conversion, following the example of John the Baptist, who prepared the way for Christ by "preaching a baptism of repentance for the forgiveness of sins" (*Mk* 1:4), as well as the example of Christ himself, who "after John was arrested, ... came into Galilee preaching the Gospel of God and saying: 'The time is fulfilled, and the kingdom of God is at hand; *repent* and believe in the Gospel' " (*Mk* 1:14-15).

Nowadays the call to conversion which missionaries address to non-Christians is put into question or passed over in silence. It is seen as an act of "proselytizing"; it is claimed that it is enough to help people to become more human or more faithful to their own religion, that it is enough to build communities capable of working for justice, freedom, peace and solidarity. What is overlooked is that every person has the right to hear the "Good News" of the God who reveals and gives himself in Christ, so that each one can live out in its fulness his or her proper calling. This lofty reality is expressed in the words of Jesus to the Samaritan woman: "If you knew the gift of God", and in the unconscious but ardent desire of the woman: "Sir, give me this water, that I may not thirst" (*Jn* 4:10, 15).

47. The Apostles, prompted by the Spirit, invited all to change their lives, to be con-

verted and to be baptized. Immediately after the event of Pentecost, Peter spoke convincingly to the crowd: "When they heard this, they were cut to the heart, and said to Peter and the rest of the Apostles, 'Brethren, what shall we do?' And Peter said to them, '*Repent*, and be baptized every one of you in the name of Jesus Christ for the forgiveness of your sins; and you shall receive the gift of the Holy Spirit' " (*Acts* 2:37-38). That very day some three thousand persons were baptized. And again, after the healing of the lame man, Peter spoke to the crowd and repeated: "*Repent* therefore, and turn again, that your sins may be blotted out!" (*Acts* 3:19).

Conversion to Christ is joined to Baptism not only because of the Church's practice, but also by the will of Christ himself, who sent the Apostles to make disciples of all nations and to baptize them (cf. *Mt* 28:19). Conversion is also joined to Baptism because of the intrinsic need to receive the fulness of new life in Christ. As Jesus says to Nicodemus: "Truly, truly, I say to you, unless one is born of water and the Spirit, he cannot enter the Kingdom of God" (*Jn* 3:5). In Baptism, in fact, we are born anew to the life of God's children, united to Jesus Christ and anointed in the Holy Spirit. Baptism is not simply a seal of conversion, a kind of external sign indicating conversion and attesting to it. Rather, it is the Sacrament which signifies and effects rebirth from the Spirit, establishes real and unbreakable bonds with the Blessed

Trinity, and makes us members of the Body of Christ, which is the Church.

All this needs to be said, since not a few people, precisely in those areas involved in the mission *ad gentes*, tend to separate conversion to Christ from Baptism, regarding Baptism as unnecessary. It is true that in some places sociological considerations associated with Baptism obscure its genuine meaning as an act of faith. This is due to a variety of historical and cultural factors which must be removed where they still exist, so that the Sacrament of spiritual rebirth can be seen for what it truly is. Local ecclesial communities must devote themselves to this task. It is also true that many profess an interior commitment to Christ and his message yet do not wish to be committed sacramentally, since, owing to prejudice or because of the failings of Christians, they find it difficult to grasp the true nature of the Church as a mystery of faith and love.[77] I wish to encourage such people to be fully open to Christ, and to remind them that, if they feel drawn to Christ, it was he himself who desired that the Church should be the "place" where they would in fact find him. At the same time, I invite the Christian faithful, both individually and as communities, to bear authentic witness to Christ through the new life they have received.

[77] Cf. SECOND VATICAN ECUMENICAL COUNCIL, Dogmatic Constitution on the Church *Lumen Gentium*, 6-9.

Certainly, every convert is a gift to the Church and represents a serious responsibility for her, not only because converts have to be prepared for Baptism through the catechumenate and then be guided by religious instruction, but also because—especially in the case of adults—such converts bring with them a kind of new energy, an enthusiasm for the faith, and a desire to see the Gospel lived out in the Church. They would be greatly disappointed if, having entered the ecclesial community, they were to find a life lacking fervour and without signs of renewal! We cannot preach conversion unless we ourselves are converted anew every day.

FORMING LOCAL CHURCHES

48.   Conversion and Baptism give entry into a Church already in existence or require the establishment of new communities which confess Jesus as Saviour and Lord. This is part of God's plan, for it pleases him "to call human beings to share in his own life not merely as individuals, without any unifying bond between them, but rather to make them into a people in which his children, who had been widely scattered, might be gathered together in unity".[78]

The mission *ad gentes* has this objective: to found Christian communities and develop

---

[78] SECOND VATICAN ECUMENICAL COUNCIL, Decree on the Missionary Activity of the Church *Ad Gentes*, 2; cf. Dogmatic Constitution on the Church *Lumen Gentium*, 9.

Churches to their full maturity. This is a central and determining goal of missionary activity, so much so that the mission is not completed until it succeeds in building a new particular Church which functions normally in its local setting. The Decree *Ad Gentes* deals with this subject at length,[79] and since the Council, a line of theological reflection has developed which emphasizes that the whole mystery of the Church is contained in each particular Church, provided it does not isolate itself but remains in communion with the universal Church and becomes missionary in its own turn. Here we are speaking of a great and lengthy process, in which it is hard to identify the precise stage at which missionary activity properly so-called comes to an end and is replaced by pastoral activity. Even so, certain points must remain clear.

49. It is necessary first and foremost to strive to establish Christian communities everywhere, communities which are "a sign of the presence of God in the world" [80] and which grow until they become Churches. Notwithstanding the high number of dioceses, there are still very large areas where there are no local Churches or where their number is insufficient in relation to the vastness of the territory and the density of the population. There

---

[79] Cf. Decree on the Missionary Activity of the Church *Ad Gentes*, Chapter III, 19-22.
[80] *Ibid.*, 15.

is still much to be done in implanting and developing the Church. This phase of ecclesial history, called the *plantatio Ecclesiae*, has not reached its end; indeed, for much of the human race it has yet to begin.

Responsibility for this task belongs to the universal Church and to the particular Churches, to the whole people of God and to all its missionary forces. Every Church, even one made up of recent converts, is missionary by its very nature, and is both evangelized and evangelizing. Faith must always be presented as a gift of God to be lived out in community (families, parishes, associations), and to be extended to others through witness in word and deed. The evangelizing activity of the Christian community, first in its own locality, and then elsewhere as part of the Church's universal mission, is the clearest sign of a mature faith. A radical conversion in thinking is required in order to become missionary, and this holds true both for individuals and entire communities. The Lord is always calling us to come out of ourselves and to share with others the goods we possess, starting with the most precious gift of all—our faith. The effectiveness of the Church's organizations, movements, parishes and apostolic works must be measured in the light of this missionary imperative. Only by becoming missionary will the Christian community be able to overcome its internal divisions and tensions, and rediscover its unity and its strength of faith.

Missionary personnel coming from other Churches and countries must work in communion with their local counterparts for the development of the Christian community. In particular, it falls to missionary personnel—in accordance with the directives of the Bishops and in cooperation with those responsible at the local level—to foster the spread of the faith and the expansion of the Church in non-Christian environments and among non-Christian groups, and to encourage a missionary sense within the particular Churches, so that pastoral concern will always be combined with concern for the mission *ad gentes*. In this way, every Church will make its own the solicitude of Christ the Good Shepherd, who fully devotes himself to his flock, but at the same time is mindful of the "other sheep, that are not of this fold" (*Jn* 10:16).

50. This solicitude will serve as a motivation and stimulus for a renewed commitment to ecumenism. The relationship between *ecumenical activity* and *missionary activity* makes it necessary to consider two closely associated factors. On the one hand, we must recognize that "the division among Christians damages the holy work of preaching the Gospel to every creature and is a barrier for many in their

approach to the faith".[81] The fact that the Good News of reconciliation is preached by Christians who are divided among themselves weakens their witness. It is thus urgent to work for the unity of Christians, so that missionary activity can be more effective. At the same time we must not forget that efforts towards unity are themselves a sign of the work of reconciliation which God is bringing about in our midst.

On the other hand, it is true that some kind of communion, though imperfect, exists among all those who have received Baptism in Christ. On this basis the Council established the principle that "while all appearance of indifferentism and confusion is ruled out, as well as any appearance of unhealthy rivalry, Catholics should collaborate in a spirit of fellowship with their separated brothers and sisters in accordance with the norms of the Decree on Ecumenism: by a common profession of faith in God and in Jesus Christ before the nations—to the extent that this is possible—and by their cooperation in social and technical as well as in cultural and religious matters".[82]

Ecumenical activity and harmonious witness to Jesus Christ by Christians who belong to different Churches and Ecclesial Communities has already borne abundant fruit. But it is ever more urgent that they work and bear wit-

---

[81] *Ibid.*, 6.
[82] *Ibid.*, 15; cf. Decree on Ecumenism *Unitatis Redintegratio*, 3.

ness together at this time when Christian and para-Christian sects are sowing confusion by their activity. The expansion of these sects represents a threat for the Catholic Church and for all the Ecclesial Communities with which she is engaged in dialogue. Wherever possible, and in the light of local circumstances, the response of Christians can itself be an ecumenical one.

"Ecclesial Basic Communities" as a Force for Evangelization

51. A rapidly growing phenomenon in the young Churches—one sometimes fostered by the Bishops and their Conferences as a pastoral priority—is that of "ecclesial basic communities" (also known by other names) which are proving to be good centres for Christian formation and missionary outreach. These are groups of Christians who, at the level of the family or in a similarly restricted setting, come together for prayer, Scripture reading, catechesis, and discussion on human and ecclesial problems with a view to a common commitment. These communities are a sign of vitality within the Church, an instrument of formation and evangelization, and a solid starting point for a new society based on a "civilization of love".

These communities decentralize and organize the parish community, to which they always remain united. They take root in less privileged and rural areas, and become a leaven of Christian life, of care for the poor and neglected, and of commitment to the transformation of society. Within them, the individual Christian experiences community and therefore senses that he or she is playing an active role and is encouraged to share in the common task. Thus, these communities become a means of evangelization and of the initial proclamation of the Gospel, and a source of new ministries. At the same time, by being imbued with Christ's love, they also show how divisions, tribalism and racism can be overcome.

Every community, if it is to be Christian, must be founded on Christ and live in him, as it listens to the word of God, focuses its prayer on the Eucharist, lives in a communion marked by oneness of heart and soul, and shares according to the needs of its members (cf. *Acts* 2:42-47). As Pope Paul VI recalled, every community must live in union with the particular and the universal Church, in heartfelt communion with the Church's Pastors and the Magisterium, with a commitment to missionary outreach and without yielding to isolationism or ideological exploitation[83]. And the Synod of Bishops stated: "Because the Church is communion, the new 'basic communities', if they truly live in unity with

---

[83] Cf. Apostolic Exhortation *Evangelii Nuntiandi*, 58: *loc. cit.*, 46-49.

the Church, are a true expression of communion and a means for the construction of a more profound communion. They are thus cause for great hope for the life of the Church".[84]

INCARNATING THE GOSPEL IN PEOPLES' CULTURES

52.   As she carries out missionary activity among the nations, the Church encounters different cultures and becomes involved in the process of inculturation. The need for such involvement has marked the Church's pilgrimage throughout her history, but today it is particularly urgent.

The process of the Church's insertion into peoples' cultures is a lengthy one. It is not a matter of purely external adaptation, for inculturation "means the intimate transformation of authentic cultural values through their integration in Christianity and the insertion of Christianity in the various human cultures".[85] The process is thus a profound and all-embracing one, which involves the Christian message and also the Church's reflection and practice. But at the same time it is a difficult process, for it must in no way compromise the distinctiveness and integrity of the Christian faith.

---

[84] Extraordinary Assembly of 1985, *Final Report,* II, C, 6.
[85] *Ibid.,* II, D, 4.

Through inculturation the Church makes the Gospel incarnate in different cultures and at the same time introduces peoples, together with their cultures, into her own community.[86] She transmits to them her own values, at the same time taking the good elements that already exist in them and renewing them from within[87]. Through inculturation the Church, for her part, becomes a more intelligible sign of what she is, and a more effective instrument of mission.

Thanks to this action within the local Churches, the universal Church herself is enriched with forms of expression and values in the various sectors of Christian life, such as evangelization, worship, theology and charitable works. She comes to know and to express better the mystery of Christ, all the while being motivated to continual renewal. During my Pastoral Visits to the young Churches I have repeatedly dealt with these themes, which are present in the Council and the subsequent Magisterium.[88]

Inculturation is a slow journey, which

[86] Cf. Apostolic Exhortation *Catechesi Tradendae* (16 October 1979), 53: *AAS* 71 (1979), 1320; Encyclical Epistle *Slavorum Apostoli* (2 June 1985), 21: *AAS* 77 (1985), 802f.

[87] Cf. PAUL VI, Apostolic Exhortation *Evangelii Nuntiandi,* 20: *loc. cit.,* 18f.

[88] *Address* to the Bishops of Zaire, Kinshasa, 3 May 1980, 4-6: *AAS* 72 (1980), 432-435; *Address* to the Bishops of Kenya, Nairobi, 7 May 1980, 6: *AAS* 72 (1980), 497; *Address* to the Bishops of India, Delhi, 1 February 1986, 5: *AAS* 78 (1986), 748f; *Homily* at Cartagena, 6 July 1986, 7-8: *AAS* 79 (1987), 105f; cf. also Encyclical Epistle *Slavorum Apostoli,* 21-22: *loc. cit.,* 802-804.

accompanies the whole of missionary life. It involves those working in the Church's mission *ad gentes,* the Christian communities as they develop, and the Bishops, who have the task of providing discernment and encouragement for its implementation.[89]

53. Missionaries, who come from other Churches and countries, must immerse themselves in the cultural milieu of those to whom they are sent, moving beyond their own cultural limitations. Hence they must learn the language of the place in which they work, become familiar with the most important expressions of the local culture, and discover its values through direct experience. Only if they have this kind of awareness will they be able to bring to people the knowledge of the hidden mystery (cf. *Rom* 16: 25-27; *Eph* 3:5) in a credible and fruitful way. It is not of course a matter of missionaries renouncing their own cultural identity, but of understanding, appreciating, fostering and evangelizing the culture of the environment in which they are working, and therefore of equipping themselves to communicate effectively with it, adopting a manner of living which is a sign of Gospel witness and of solidarity with the people.

Developing ecclesial communities, inspired by the Gospel, will gradually be able to express

---

[89] Cf. SECOND VATICAN ECUMENICAL COUNCIL, Decree on the Missionary Activity of the Church *Ad Gentes,* 22.

their Christian experience in original ways and forms that are consonant with their own cultural traditions, provided that those traditions are in harmony with the objective requirements of the faith itself. To this end, especially in the more delicate areas of inculturation, particular Churches of the same region should work in communion with each other [90] and with the whole Church, convinced that only through attention both to the universal Church and to the particular Churches will they be capable of translating the treasure of faith into a legitimate variety of expressions.[91] Groups which have been evangelized will thus provide the elements for a "translation" of the Gospel message,[92] keeping in mind the positive elements acquired down the centuries from Christianity's contact with different cultures and not forgetting the dangers of alterations which have sometimes occurred.[93]

54. In this regard, certain guidelines remain basic. Properly applied, inculturation must be guided by two principles: "compatibility with

---

[90] Cf. *ibid.*

[91] Cf. PAUL VI, Apostolic Exhortation *Evangelii Nuntiandi,* 64: *loc. cit.,* 55.

[92] *Ibid.,* 63: *loc. cit.,* 53: Particular Churches "have the task of assimilating the essence of the Gospel message and of transposing it, without the slightest betrayal of its essential truth, into the language that these people understand, then of proclaiming it in this language ... And the word 'language' should be understood here less in the semantic or literary sense than in the sense which one may call anthropological or cultural".

[93] Cf. *Address* at the General Audience of 13 April 1988: *Insegnamenti* XI/I (1988), 877-881.

the Gospel and communion with the universal Church".[94] Bishops, as guardians of the "deposit of faith", will take care to ensure fidelity and, in particular, to provide discernment,[95] for which a deeply balanced approach is required. In fact there is a risk of passing uncritically from a form of alienation from culture to an overestimation of culture. Since culture is a human creation and is therefore marked by sin, it too needs to be "healed, ennobled and perfected".[96]

This kind of process needs to take place gradually, in such a way that it really is an expression of the community's Christian experience. As Pope Paul VI said in Kampala: "it will require an incubation of the Christian 'mystery' in the genius of your people in order that its native voice, more clearly and frankly, may then be raised harmoniously in the chorus of other voices in the universal Church".[97] In effect, inculturation must involve the whole people of God, and not just a few experts, since the people reflect the authentic "sensus fidei" which must never be lost sight of. Inculturation needs to be guided and encouraged, but not forced, lest it give rise to negative reac-

[94] Apostolic Exhortation *Familiaris Consortio* (22 November 1981), 10: *AAS* 74 (1982), 91, which speaks of inculturation "in the context of marriage and the family".

[95] Cf. PAUL VI, Apostolic Exhortation *Evangelii Nuntiandi*, 63-65: *loc. cit.,* 53-56.

[96] SECOND VATICAN ECUMENICAL COUNCIL, Dogmatic Constitution on the Church *Lumen Gentium,* 17.

[97] *Address* to those participating in the Symposium of African Bishops at Kampala, 31 July 1969, 2: *AAS* 61 (1969), 577.

tions among Christians. It must be an expression of the community's life, one which must mature within the community itself, and not be exclusively the result of erudite research. The safeguarding of traditional values is the work of a mature faith.

DIALOGUE WITH OUR BROTHERS AND SISTERS OF OTHER RELIGIONS

55. Inter-religious dialogue is a part of the Church's evangelizing mission. Understood as a method and means of mutual knowledge and enrichment, dialogue is not in opposition to the mission *ad gentes;* indeed, it has special links with that mission and is one of its expressions. This mission, in fact, is addressed to those who do not know Christ and his Gospel, and who belong for the most part to other religions. In Christ, God calls all peoples to himself and he wishes to share with them the fulness of his revelation and love. He does not fail to make himself present in many ways, not only to individuals but also to entire peoples through their spiritual riches, of which their religions are the main and essential expression, even when they contain "gaps, insufficiencies and errors".[98] All of this has been given ample

---

[98] PAUL VI, *Address* at the opening of the Second Session of the Second Vatican Ecumenical Council, 29 September 1963: *AAS* 55 (1963), 858; cf. SECOND VATICAN ECUMENICAL COUNCIL, Declaration on the Church's Relation to Non-Christian Religions *Nostra Aetate*, 2; Dogmatic Constitution on the Church *Lumen Gentium*, 16; Decree on the Missionary Activity of the

emphasis by the Council and the subsequent Magisterium, without detracting in any way from the fact that *salvation comes from Christ and that dialogue does not dispense from evangelization.*[99]

In the light of the economy of salvation, the Church sees no conflict between proclaiming Christ and engaging in inter-religious dialogue. Instead, she feels the need to link the two in the context of her mission *ad gentes*. These two elements must maintain both their intimate connection and their distinctiveness; therefore they should not be confused, manipulated or regarded as identical, as though they were interchangeable.

I recently wrote to the Bishops of Asia: "Although the Church gladly acknowledges whatever is true and holy in the religious traditions of Buddhism, Hinduism and Islam as a reflection of that truth which enlightens all men, this does not lessen her duty and resolve to proclaim without fail Jesus Christ who is 'the way, and the truth and the life' ... The fact that the followers of other religions can receive God's grace and be saved by Christ apart from the ordinary means which he has established does not thereby cancel the call to

Church *Ad Gentes*, 9; PAUL VI, Apostolic Exhortation *Evangelii Nuntiandi*, 53: *loc. cit.*, 41f.

[99] Cf. PAUL VI, Encyclical Letter *Ecclesiam Suam* (6 August 1964): *AAS* 56 (1964), 609-659; SECOND VATICAN ECUMENICAL COUNCIL, Decree on the Missionary Activity of the Church *Ad Gentes*, 11, 41; SECRETARIAT FOR NON-CHRISTIANS, Document *L'atteggiamento della Chiesa di fronte ai seguaci di altre religioni: Riflessioni e orientamenti su dialogo e missione* (4 September 1984): *AAS* 76 (1984), 816-828.

faith and baptism which God wills for all people".[100] Indeed Christ himself "while expressly insisting on the need for faith and baptism, at the same time confirmed *the need for the Church,* into which people enter through Baptism as through a door".[101] Dialogue should be conducted and implemented with the conviction that *the Church is the ordinary means of salvation* and that *she alone* possesses the fulness of the means of salvation.[102]

56.   Dialogue does not originate from tactical concerns or self-interest, but is an activity with its own guiding principles, requirements and dignity. It is demanded by deep respect for everything that has been brought about in human beings by the Spirit who blows where he wills.[103] Through dialogue, the Church seeks to uncover the "seeds of the Word",[104] a "ray of that truth which enlightens all men";[105] these are found in individuals and in the religious traditions of mankind. Dialogue is based on hope and love, and will bear fruit in the Spirit.

[100] *Letter* to the Fifth Plenary Assembly of Asian Bishops' Conferences (23 June 1990), 4: *L'Osservatore Romano,* 18 July 1990.
[101] SECOND VATICAN ECUMENICAL COUNCIL, Dogmatic Constitution on the Church *Lumen Gentium,* 14; cf. Decree on the Missionary Activity of the Church *Ad Gentes,* 7.
[102] Cf. SECOND VATICAN ECUMENICAL COUNCIL, Decree on Ecumenism *Unitatis Redintegratio,* 3; Decree on the Missionary Activity of the Church *Ad Gentes,* 7.
[103] Cf. Encyclical Letter *Redemptor Hominis,* 12: *loc. cit.,* 279.
[104] SECOND VATICAN ECUMENICAL COUNCIL, Decree on the Missionary Activity of the Church *Ad Gentes,* 11, 15.
[105] SECOND VATICAN ECUMENICAL COUNCIL, Declaration on the Church's Relation to Non-Christian Religions *Nostra Aetate,* 2.

Other religions constitute a positive challenge for the Church: they stimulate her both to discover and acknowledge the signs of Christ's presence and of the working of the Spirit, as well as to examine more deeply her own identity and to bear witness to the fulness of Revelation which she has received for the good of all.

This gives rise to the spirit which must enliven dialogue in the context of mission. Those engaged in this dialogue must be consistent with their own religious traditions and convictions, and be open to understanding those of the other party without pretence or close-mindedness, but with truth, humility and frankness, knowing that dialogue can enrich each side. There must be no abandonment of principles nor false irenicism, but instead a witness given and received for mutual advancement on the road of religious inquiry and experience, and at the same time for the elimination of prejudice, intolerance and misunderstandings. Dialogue leads to inner purification and conversion which, if pursued with docility to the Holy Spirit, will be spiritually fruitful.

57.   A vast field lies open to dialogue, which can assume many forms and expressions: from exchanges between experts in religious traditions or official representatives of those traditions to cooperation for integral development and the safeguarding of religious values;

and from a sharing of their respective spiritual experiences to the so-called "dialogue of life", through which believers of different religions bear witness before each other in daily life to their own human and spiritual values, and help each other to live according to those values in order to build a more just and fraternal society.

Each member of the faithful and all Christian communities are called to practise dialogue, although not always to the same degree or in the same way. The contribution of the laity is indispensable in this area, for they "can favour the relations which ought to be established with the followers of various religions through their example in the situations in which they live and in their activities". [106] Some of them also will be able to make a contribution through research and study. [107]

I am well aware that many missionaries and Christian communities find in the difficult and often misunderstood path of dialogue their only way of bearing sincere witness to Christ and offering generous service to others. I wish to encourage them to persevere with faith and love, even in places where their efforts are not well received. Dialogue is a path towards the Kingdom and will certainly bear fruit, even if the times and seasons are known only to the Father (cf. *Acts* 1:7).

---

[106] Apostolic Exhortation *Christifideles Laici*, 35: *loc. cit.*, 458.

[107] Cf. SECOND VATICAN ECUMENICAL COUNCIL, Decree on the Missionary Activity of the Church *Ad Gentes*, 41.

58.   The mission *ad gentes* is still being carried out today, for the most part in the
southern regions of the world, where action on
behalf of integral development and liberation
from all forms of oppression is most urgently
needed. The Church has always been able to
generate among the peoples she evangelizes a
drive towards progress. Today, more than in
the past, missionaries are being recognized as
promoters of development by governments and international experts, who are impressed at the
remarkable results achieved with scanty means.

In the Encyclical *Sollicitudo Rei Socialis,* I
stated that "the Church does not have technical
solutions to offer for the problem of underdevelopment as such", but "offers her first contribution to the solution of the urgent problem
of development when she proclaims the truth
about Christ, about herself and about man,
applying this truth to a concrete situation".[108]
The Conference of Latin American Bishops at
Puebla stated that "the best service we can offer
to our brother is evangelization, which helps
him to live and act as a son of God, sets him
free from injustices and assists his overall development".[109] It is not the Church's mission

---

[108] Encyclical Letter *Sollicitudo Rei Socialis* (30 December 1987),
41: *AAS* 80 (1988), 570f.
[109] *Documents* of the Third General Conference of Latin American Bishops, Puebla (1979), 3760 (1145).

to work directly on the economic, technical or political levels, or to contribute materially to development. Rather, her mission consists essentially in offering people an opportunity not to "have more" but to "be more", by awakening their consciences through the Gospel. "Authentic human development must be rooted in an ever deeper evangelization".[110]

The Church and her missionaries also promote development through schools, hospitals, printing presses, universities and experimental farms. But a people's development does not derive primarily from money, material assistance or technological means, but from the formation of consciences and the gradual maturing of ways of thinking and patterns of behaviour. *Man is the principal agent of development,* not money or technology. The Church forms consciences by revealing to peoples the God whom they seek and do not yet know, the grandeur of man created in God's image and loved by him, the equality of all men and women as God's sons and daughters, the mastery of man over nature created by God and placed at man's service, and the obligation to work for the development of the whole person and of all mankind.

59. Through the Gospel message, the Church offers a force for liberation which promotes development precisely because it

---

[110] *Address* to Clergy and Religious, Jakarta, 10 October 1989, 5: *L'Osservatore Romano,* 11 October 1989.

leads to conversion of heart and of ways of thinking, fosters the recognition of each person's dignity, encourages solidarity, commitment and service of one's neighbour, and gives everyone a place in God's plan, which is the building of his Kingdom of peace and justice, beginning already in this life. This is the Biblical perspective of the "new heavens and a new earth" (cf. *Is* 65:17; *2 Pt* 3:13; *Rev* 21:1), which has been the stimulus and goal for mankind's advancement in history. Man's development derives from God, from the model of Jesus—God and man—and must lead back to God.[111] That is why there is a close connection between the proclamation of the Gospel and human promotion.

The contribution of the Church and of evangelization to the development of peoples concerns not only the struggle against material poverty and underdevelopment in the South of the world, but also concerns the North, which is prone to a moral and spiritual poverty caused by "overdevelopment".[112] A certain way of thinking, uninfluenced by a religious outlook and widespread in some parts of today's world, is based on the idea that increasing wealth and the promotion of economic and technical growth is enough for people to develop on

[111] Cf. PAUL VI, Encyclical Letter *Populorum Progressio*, 14-21, 40-42: *loc. cit.*, 264-268, 277f; JOHN PAUL II, Encyclical Letter *Sollicitudo Rei Socialis*, 27-41: *loc. cit.*, 547-572.
[112] Cf. Encyclical Letter *Sollicitudo Rei Socialis*, 28: *loc. cit.*, 548-550.

the human level. But a soulless development cannot suffice for human beings, and an excess of affluence is as harmful as excessive poverty. This is a "development model" which the North has constructed and is now spreading to the South, where a sense of religion as well as human values are in danger of being overwhelmed by a wave of consumerism.

"Fight hunger by changing your lifestyle" is a motto which has appeared in Church circles and which shows the people of the rich nations how to become brothers and sisters of the poor. We need to turn to a more austere way of life which will favour a new model of development that gives attention to ethical and religious values. To the poor, *missionary activity* brings light and an impulse towards true development, while a new evangelization ought to create among the wealthy a realization that the time has arrived for them to become true brothers and sisters of the poor through the conversion of all to an "integral development" open to the Absolute.[113]

CHARITY: SOURCE AND CRITERION OF MISSION

60.   As I said during my Pastoral Visit to Brazil: "The Church all over the world wishes to be the Church of the poor ... she wishes to

[113] Cf. *ibid.*, Chap. IV, 27-34: *loc. cit.*, 547-560; PAUL VI, Encyclical Letter *Populorum Progressio*, 19-21, 41-42: *loc. cit.*, 266-268, 277f.

draw out all the truth contained in the Beatitudes of Christ, and especially in the first one: 'Blessed are the poor in spirit' ... She wishes to teach this truth and she wishes to put it into practice, just as Jesus came to do and to teach".[114]

The young Churches, which for the most part are to be found among peoples suffering from widespread poverty, often give voice to this concern as an integral part of their mission. The Conference of Latin American Bishops at Puebla, after recalling the example of Jesus, wrote that "the poor deserve preferential attention, whatever their moral or personal situation. They have been made in the image and likeness of God to be his children, but this image has been obscured and even violated. For this reason, God has become their defender and loves them. It follows that the poor are those to whom the mission is first addressed, and their evangelization is *par excellence* the sign and proof of the mission of Jesus".[115]

In fidelity to the spirit of the Beatitudes, the Church is called to be on the side of those who are poor and oppressed in any way. I therefore exhort the disciples of Christ and all Christian communities—from families to dioceses, from parishes to Religious Institutes—to carry out a sincere review of their lives regard-

---

[114] *Address* to the residents of "Favela Vidigal" in Rio de Janeiro, 2 July 1980, 4: *AAS* 72 (1980), 854.
[115] *Documents* of the Third General Conference of Latin American Bishops, Puebla, (1979), 3757 (1142).

ing their solidarity with the poor. At the same time, I express gratitude to the missionaries who, by their loving presence and humble service to people, are working for the integral development of individuals and of society through schools, health-care centres, leprosaria, homes for the handicapped and the elderly, projects for the promotion of women, and other similar apostolates. I thank the priests, religious Brothers and Sisters, and members of the laity for their dedication, and I also encourage the volunteers from non-governmental organizations who in ever increasing numbers are devoting themselves to works of charity and human promotion.

It is in fact these "works of charity" that reveal the soul of all missionary activity: *love,* which has been and remains *the driving force of mission,* and is also "the sole criterion for judging what is to be done or not done, changed or not changed. It is the principle which must direct every action, and the end to which that action must be directed. When we act with a view to charity, or are inspired by charity, nothing is unseemly and everything is good". [116]

---

[116] ISAAC OF STELLA, *Sermon* 31, PL 194, 1793.

CHAPTER VI

LEADERS AND WORKERS
IN THE MISSIONARY APOSTOLATE

61. Without witnesses there can be no witness, just as without missionaries there can be no missionary activity. Jesus chooses and sends people forth to be his witnesses and apostles, so that they may share in his mission and continue his saving work: "You shall be my witnesses in Jerusalem and in all Judea and Samaria and to the end of the earth" (*Acts* 1:8).

The Twelve are the first to work in the Church's universal mission. They constitute a "collegial subject" of that mission, having been chosen by Jesus to be with him and to be sent forth "to the lost sheep of the house of Israel" (*Mt* 10:6). This collegiality does not prevent certain figures from assuming prominence within the group, such as James, John and above all Peter, who is so prominent as to justify the expression: "Peter and the other Apostles" (*Acts* 2:14, 37). It was thanks to Peter that the horizons of the Church's universal mission were expanded, and the way was prepared for the outstanding missionary work of Paul, who by God's will was called and sent forth to the nations (cf. *Gal* 1:15-16).

In the early Church's missionary expansion, we find, alongside the Apostles, other lesser figures who should not be overlooked. These include individuals, groups and communities. A typical example is the local Church at Antioch which, after being evangelized, becomes an evangelizing community which sends missionaries to others (cf. *Acts* 13:2-3). The early Church experiences her mission as a community task, while acknowledging in her midst certain "special envoys" or "missionaries devoted to the Gentiles", such as Paul and Barnabas.

62. What was done at the beginning of Christianity to further its universal mission remains valid and urgent today. *The Church is missionary by her very nature,* for Christ's mandate is not something contingent or external, but reaches the very heart of the Church. It follows that the universal Church and each individual Church is sent forth to the nations. Precisely "so that this missionary zeal may flourish among the people of their own country", it is highly appropriate that young Churches should "share as soon as possible in the universal missionary work of the Church. They should themselves send missionaries to proclaim the Gospel all over the world, even though they are suffering from a shortage of

clergy".[117] Many are already doing so, and I strongly encourage them to continue.

In this essential bond between the universal Church and the particular Churches the authentic and full missionary nature of the Church finds practical expression: "In a world where the lessening of distance makes the world increasingly smaller, the Church's communities ought to be connected with each other, exchange vital energies and resources, and commit themselves as a group to the one and common mission of proclaiming and living the Gospel ... So-called younger Churches have need of the strength of the older Churches and the older ones need the witness and the impulse of the younger, so that each Church can draw on the riches of the other Churches".[118]

THOSE PRIMARILY RESPONSIBLE FOR MISSIONARY ACTIVITY

63. Just as the Risen Lord gave the universal missionary mandate to the College of the Apostles with Peter as its head, so this same responsibility now rests primarily with the College of Bishops, headed by the Successor of Peter.[119] Conscious of this responsibility, I

---

[117] SECOND VATICAN ECUMENICAL COUNCIL, Decree on the Missionary Activity of the Church *Ad Gentes*, 20.

[118] Apostolic Exhortation *Christifideles Laici*, 35: *loc. cit.*, 458.

[119] Cf. SECOND VATICAN ECUMENICAL COUNCIL, Decree on the Missionary Activity of the Church *Ad Gentes*, 38.

feel the duty to give expression to it in my meetings with the Bishops, both with regard to new evangelization and the universal mission. I have travelled all over the world in order "to proclaim the Gospel, to 'strengthen the brothers' in the faith, to console the Church, to meet people. They are journeys of faith ... they are likewise opportunities for travelling catechesis, for evangelical proclamation in spreading the Gospel and the apostolic Magisterium to the full extent of the world".[120]

My brother Bishops are directly responsible, together with me, for the evangelization of the world, both as members of the College of Bishops and as Pastors of the particular Churches. In this regard the Council states: "The charge of announcing the Gospel throughout the world belongs to the body of shepherds, to all of whom in common Christ gave the command".[121] It also stated that the Bishops "have been consecrated not only for a particular diocese but for the salvation of the entire world".[122] This collegial responsibility has certain practical consequences. Thus, "the Synod of Bishops ... should, among the concerns of general importance, pay special attention to missionary activity, the greatest and holiest

---

[120] *Address* to Cardinals and those associated in the work of the Roman Curia, Vatican City and the Vicariate of Rome, 28 June 1980, 10: *Insegnamenti,* III/1 (1980), 1887.

[121] Dogmatic Constitution on the Church *Lumen Gentium,* 23.

[122] Decree on the Missionary Activity of the Church *Ad Gentes,* 38.

duty of the Church".[123] The same responsibility is reflected to varying degrees in Episcopal Conferences and their organisms at a continental level, which must make their own contribution to the missionary task.[124]

Each Bishop too, as the Pastor of a particular Church, has a wide-ranging missionary duty. It falls to him "as the ruler and centre of unity in the diocesan apostolate, to promote missionary activity, to direct and coordinate it ... Let him also see to it that apostolic activity is not limited only to those who are already converted, but that a fair share both of personnel and funds be devoted to the evangelization of non-Christians".[125]

64.   Each particular Church must be generous and open to the needs of the other Churches. Cooperation between the Churches, in an authentic reciprocity that prepares them both to give and to receive, is a source of enrichment for all of them and touches the various spheres of ecclesial life. In this respect, the declaration of the Bishops at Puebla is exemplary: "The hour has finally come for Latin America ... to be projected beyond her frontiers, *ad gentes*. Certainly we have need of missionaries ourselves, nevertheless we must give from our own poverty".[126]

---

[123] *Ibid.,* 29.
[124] Cf. *ibid.,* 38.
[125] *Ibid.,* 30.
[126] *Documents* of the Third General Conference of Latin American Bishops, Puebla (1979): 2941 (368).

In the same spirit, I exhort Bishops and Episcopal Conferences to act generously in implementing the provisions of the *Norms* which the Congregation for the Clergy issued regarding cooperation between particular Churches and especially regarding the better distribution of clergy in the world.[127]

The Church's mission is wider than the "communion among the Churches"; it ought to be directed not only to aiding re-evangelization but also and primarily to missionary activity as such. I appeal to all the Churches, young and old alike, to share in this concern of mine by seeking to overcome the various obstacles and increase missionary vocations.

MISSIONARIES AND RELIGIOUS INSTITUTES
AD GENTES

65. Now, as in the past, among those involved in the missionary apostolate a place of fundamental importance is held by the persons and institutions to whom the Decree *Ad Gentes* devotes the special chapter entitled "Missionaries".[128] This requires careful reflection, especially on the part of missionaries themselves, who may be led, as a result of changes occurring within the missionary field, no longer to

---

[127] Cf. Norms for the Cooperation of the Local Churches among Themselves and especially for a Better Distribution of the Clergy in the World *Postquam Apostoli* (25 March 1980): *AAS* 72 (1980), 343-364.
[128] Cf. Decree on the Missionary Activity of the Church *Ad Gentes*, Chapter IV, 23-27.

understand the meaning of their vocation and no longer to know exactly what the Church expects of them today.

The following words of the Council are a point of reference: "Although the task of spreading the faith, to the best of one's ability, falls to each disciple of Christ, the Lord always calls from the number of his disciples those whom he wishes, so that they may be with him and that he may send them to preach to the nations. Accordingly, through the Holy Spirit, who distributes his gifts as he wishes for the good of all, Christ stirs up a missionary vocation in the hearts of individuals, and at the same time raises up in the Church those Institutes which undertake the duty of evangelization, which is the responsibility of the whole Church, as their special task".[129]

What is involved, therefore, is a "special vocation", patterned on that of the Apostles. It is manifested in a total commitment to evangelization, a commitment which involves the missionary's whole person and life, and demands a self-giving without limits of energy or time. Those who have received this vocation, "sent by legitimate authority, go out, in faith and obedience, to those who are far from Christ, set aside for the work to which they have been called as ministers of the Gospel".[130] Missionaries must always meditate on

<hr />

[129] *Ibid.*, 23.
[130] *Ibid.*

the response demanded by the gift they have received, and continually keep their doctrinal and apostolic formation up to date.

66. Missionary Institutes, drawing from their experience and creativity while remaining faithful to their founding charism, must employ all means necessary to ensure the adequate preparation of candidates and the renewal of their members' spiritual, moral and physical energies.[131] They should sense that they are a vital part of the ecclesial community and should carry out their work in communion with it. Indeed, "every Institute exists for the Church and must enrich her with its distinctive characteristics, according to a particular spirit and a specific mission"; the guardians of this fidelity to the founding charism are the Bishops themselves.[132]

In general, Missionary Institutes came into being in Churches located in traditionally Christian countries, and historically they have been the means employed by the Congregation of *Propaganda Fide* for the spread of the faith and the founding of new Churches. Today, these Institutes are receiving more and more candidates from the young Churches

---

[131] *Ibid.*, 23, 27.

[132] Cf. SACRED CONGREGATION FOR RELIGIOUS AND SECULAR INSTITUTES and SACRED CONGREGATION FOR BISHOPS, Directives for Mutual Relations between Bishops and Religious in the Church *Mutuae Relationes* (14 May 1978), 14b: *AAS* 70 (1978), 482; cf. n. 28: *loc. cit.*, 490.

which they founded, while new Missionary Institutes have arisen in countries which previously only received missionaries, but are now also sending them. This is a praiseworthy trend which demonstrates the continuing validity and relevance of the specific missionary vocation of these Institutes. They remain "absolutely necessary",[133] not only for missionary activity *ad gentes,* in keeping with their tradition, but also for stirring up missionary fervour both in the Churches of traditionally Christian countries and in the younger Churches.

The special vocation of missionaries *"for life"* retains all its validity: it is the model of the Church's missionary commitment, which always stands in need of radical and total self-giving, of new and bold endeavours. Therefore the men and women missionaries who have devoted their whole lives to bearing witness to the Risen Lord among the nations must not allow themselves to be daunted by doubts, misunderstanding, rejection or persecution. They should revive the grace of their specific charism and courageously press on, preferring—in a spirit of faith, obedience and communion with their Pastors—to seek the lowliest and most demanding places.

---

[133] SECOND VATICAN ECUMENICAL COUNCIL, Decree on the Missionary Activity of the Church *Ad Gentes,* 27.

67.   As co-workers of the Bishops, priests are called by virtue of the Sacrament of Orders to share in concern for the Church's mission: "The spiritual gift that priests have received in ordination prepares them, not for any narrow and limited mission, but for *the most universal and all-embracing mission of salvation* 'to the end of the earth'. For every priestly ministry shares in the universal scope of the mission that Christ entrusted to his Apostles".[134] For this reason, the formation of candidates to the priesthood must aim at giving them *"the true Catholic spirit,* whereby they will learn to transcend the bounds of their own diocese, country or rite, and come to the aid of the whole Church, in readiness to preach the Gospel anywhere".[135] All priests must have the mind and heart of missionaries—open to the needs of the Church and the world, with concern for those farthest away, and especially for the non-Christian groups in their own area. They should have at heart, in their prayers and particularly at the Eucharistic Sacrifice, the concern of the whole Church for all of humanity.

[134] SECOND VATICAN ECUMENICAL COUNCIL, Decree on the Ministry and Life of Priests *Presbyterorum Ordinis,* 10; cf. Decree on the Missionary Activity of the Church *Ad Gentes,* 39.

[135] SECOND VATICAN ECUMENICAL COUNCIL, Decree on Priestly Formation *Optatam Totius,* 20: cf. "Guide de la vie pastorale pour les prêtres diocésains des Eglises qui dependent de la Congrégation pour l'Evangélisation des Peuples", Rome, 1989.

Especially in those areas where Christians are a minority, priests must be filled with special missionary zeal and commitment. The Lord entrusts to them not only the pastoral care of the Christian community, but also and above all the evangelization of those of their fellow-citizens who do not belong to Christ's flock. Priests will "not fail to make themselves readily available to the Holy Spirit and the Bishop, to be sent to preach the Gospel beyond the borders of their country. This will demand of them not only maturity in their vocation, but also an uncommon readiness to detach themselves from their own homeland, culture and family, and a special ability to adapt to other cultures, with understanding and respect for them".[136]

68. In his Encyclical *Fidei Donum*, Pope Pius XII, with prophetic insight, encouraged Bishops to offer some of their priests for temporary service in the Churches of Africa, and gave his approval to projects already existing for that purpose. Twenty-five years later, I pointed out the striking newness of that Encyclical, which "surmounted the territorial dimension of priestly service in order to direct it towards the entire Church".[137] Today it is clear how effective and fruitful this experience has

---

[136] *Address* to the Plenary Assembly of the Congregation for the Evangelization of Peoples, 14 April 1989, 4: *AAS* 81 (1989), 1140.
[137] *Message* for World Mission Day, 1982: *Insegnamenti* V/2 (1982), 1879.

been. Indeed, *Fidei Donum* priests are a unique sign of the bond of communion existing among the Churches. They make a valuable contribution to the growth of needy ecclesial communities, while drawing from them freshness and liveliness of faith. Of course, the missionary service of the diocesan priest must conform to certain criteria and conditions. The priests to be sent should be selected from among the most suitable candidates, and should be duly prepared for the particular work that awaits them.[138] With an open and fraternal attitude, they should become part of the new setting of the Church which welcomes them, and form one presbyterate with the local priests, under the authority of the Bishop.[139] I hope that a spirit of service will increase among the priests of the long-established Churches, and that it will be fostered among priests of the Churches of more recent origin.

THE MISSIONARY FRUITFULNESS OF CONSECRATED LIFE

69. From the inexhaustible and manifold richness of the Spirit come the vocations of the

---

[138] Cf. SECOND VATICAN ECUMENICAL COUNCIL, Decree on the Missionary Activity of the Church *Ad Gentes,* 38; SACRED CONGREGATION FOR THE CLERGY, Norms *Postquam Apostoli,* 24-25: *loc. cit.,* 361.

[139] Cf. SACRED CONGREGATION FOR THE CLERGY, Norms *Postquam Apostoli,* 29: *loc. cit.,* 362f; SECOND VATICAN ECUMENICAL COUNCIL, Decree on the Missionary Activity of the Church *Ad Gentes,* 20.

Institutes of Consecrated Life, whose members, "because of the dedication to the service of the Church deriving from their very consecration, have an obligation to play a special part in missionary activity, in a manner appropriate to their Institute".[140] History witnesses to the outstanding service rendered by Religious Families in the spread of the faith and the formation of new Churches: from the ancient monastic institutions, to the medieval Orders, up to the more recent Congregations.

(*a*) Echoing the Council, I invite *Institutes of Contemplative Life* to establish communities in the young Churches, so as to "bear glorious witness among non-Christians to the majesty and love of God, as well as to unity in Christ".[141] This presence is beneficial throughout the non-Christian world, especially in those areas where religious traditions hold the contemplative life in great esteem for its asceticism and its search for the Absolute.

(*b*) To *Institutes of Active Life,* I would recommend the immense opportunities for works of charity, for the proclamation of the Gospel, for Christian education, cultural endeavours and solidarity with the poor and those suffering from discrimination, abandonment and oppression. Whether they pursue a strictly missionary goal or not, such Institutes

---

[140] *CIC,* c. 783.
[141] Decree on the Missionary Activity of the Church *Ad Gentes,* 40.

117

should ask themselves how willing and able they are to broaden their action in order to extend God's Kingdom. In recent times many Institutes have responded to this request, which I hope will be given even greater consideration and implementation for a more authentic service. The Church needs to make known the great Gospel values of which she is the bearer. No one witnesses more effectively to these values than those who profess the consecrated life in chastity, poverty and obedience, in a total gift of self to God and in complete readiness to serve man and society after the example of Christ.[142]

70. I extend a special word of appreciation to the missionary Religious Sisters, in whom virginity for the sake of the Kingdom is transformed into a motherhood in the spirit that is rich and fruitful. It is precisely the mission *ad gentes* that offers them vast scope for "the gift of self with love in a total and undivided manner".[143] The example and activity of women who through virginity are consecrated to love of God and neighbour, especially the very poor, are an indispensable evangelical sign among those peoples and cultures where women still have far to go on the way towards human promotion and liberation. It is my hope that many

[142] Cf. PAUL VI, Apostolic Exhortation *Evangelii Nuntiandi*, 69: *loc. cit.*, 58f.
[143] Apostolic Letter *Mulieris Dignitatem* (15 August 1988), 20: *AAS* 80 (1988), 1703.

young Christian women will be attracted to giving themselves generously to Christ, and will draw strength and joy from their consecration in order to bear witness to him among the peoples who do not know him.

ALL THE LAITY
ARE MISSIONARIES BY BAPTISM

71. Recent Popes have stressed the importance of the role of the laity in missionary activity.[144] In the Exhortation *Christifideles Laici,* I spoke explicitly of the Church's "permanent mission of bringing the Gospel to the multitudes—the millions and millions of men and women—who as yet do not know Christ the Redeemer of humanity",[145] and of the responsibility of the lay faithful in this regard. The mission *ad gentes* is incumbent upon the entire People of God. Whereas the foundation of a new Church requires the Eucharist and hence the priestly ministry, missionary activity, which is carried out in a wide variety of ways, is the task of all the Christian faithful.

It is clear that from the very origins of Christianity, the laity—as individuals, families, and entire communities—shared in spreading the faith. Pope Pius XII recalled this fact in his

---

[144] Cf. PIUS XII, Encyclical Letter *Evangelii Praecones: loc. cit.,* 510ff; Encyclical Letter *Fidei Donum: loc. cit.,* 228ff; JOHN XXIII, Encyclical Letter *Princeps Pastorum: loc. cit.,* 855ff; PAUL VI, Apostolic Exhortation *Evangelii Nuntiandi,* 70-73: *loc. cit.,* 59-63.

[145] Apostolic Exhortation *Christifideles Laici,* 35: *loc. cit.,* 457.

first Encyclical on the missions,[146] in which he pointed out some instances of lay missions. In modern times, this active participation of lay men and women missionaries has not been lacking. How can we forget the important role played by women: their work in the family, in schools, in political, social and cultural life, and especially their teaching of Christian doctrine? Indeed, it is necessary to recognize—and it is a title of honour—that some Churches owe their origins to the activity of lay men and women missionaries.

The Second Vatican Council confirmed this tradition in its description of the missionary character of the entire People of God and of the apostolate of the laity in particular,[147] emphasizing the specific contribution to missionary activity which they are called to make.[148] The need for all the faithful to share in this responsibility is not merely a matter of making the apostolate more effective; it is a right and duty based on their baptismal dignity, whereby "the faithful participate, for their part, in the threefold mission of Christ as Priest, Prophet and King".[149] Therefore, "they are bound by the general obligation and they have the right, whether as individuals or in associations, to strive so that the divine message of

---

[146] Cf. Encyclical Letter *Evangelii Praecones: loc. cit.*, 510-514.

[147] Cf. Dogmatic Constitution on the Church *Lumen Gentium*, 17, 33ff.

[148] Cf. Decree on the Missionary Activity of the Church *Ad Gentes*, 35-36, 41.

[149] Apostolic Exhortation *Christifideles Laici*, 14: *loc. cit.*, 410.

120

salvation may be known and accepted by all people throughout the world. This obligation is all the more insistent in circumstances in which only through them are people able to hear the Gospel and to know Christ".[150] Furthermore, because of their secular character, they especially are called "to seek the Kingdom of God by engaging in temporal affairs and ordering these in accordance with the will of God".[151]

72. The sphere in which lay people are present and active as missionaries is very extensive. "Their own field ... is the vast and complicated world of politics, society and economics ..." [152] on the local, national and international levels. Within the Church, there are various types of services, functions, ministries and ways of promoting the Christian life. I call to mind, as a new development occurring in many Churches in recent times, the rapid growth of "ecclesial movements" filled with missionary dynamism. When these movements humbly seek to become part of the life of local Churches and are welcomed by Bishops and priests within diocesan and parish structures, they represent a true gift of God both

---

[150] *CIC*, c. 225, 1; cf. SECOND VATICAN ECUMENICAL COUNCIL, Decree on the Apostolate of the Laity *Apostolicam Actuositatem*, 6, 13.

[151] SECOND VATICAN ECUMENICAL COUNCIL, Dogmatic Constitution on the Church *Lumen Gentium*, 31; cf. *CIC*, c. 225, 2.

[152] PAUL VI, Apostolic Exhortation *Evangelii Nuntiandi*, 70: *loc. cit.*, 60.

for new evangelization and for missionary activity properly so-called. I therefore recommend that they be spread, and that they be used to give fresh energy, especially among young people, to the Christian life and to evangelization, within a pluralistic view of the ways in which Christians can associate and express themselves.

Within missionary activity, the different forms of the lay apostolate should be held in esteem, with respect for their nature and aims. Lay missionary associations, international Christian volunteer organizations, ecclesial movements, groups and sodalities of different kinds—all these should be involved in the mission *ad gentes* as cooperators with the local Churches. In this way the growth of a mature and responsible laity will be fostered, a laity whom the younger Churches are recognizing as "an essential and undeniable element in the *plantatio Ecclesiae*".[153]

THE WORK OF CATECHISTS
AND THE VARIETY OF MINISTRIES

73.   Among the laity who become evangelizers, catechists have a place of honour. The Decree on the Missionary Activity of the Church speaks of them as "that army of catechists, both men and women, worthy of praise, to whom missionary work among the

---

[153] Apostolic Exhortation *Christifideles Laici*, 35: *loc. cit.*, 458.

nations owes so much. Imbued with the apostolic spirit, they make a singular and absolutely necessary contribution to the spread of the faith and of the Church by their strenuous efforts".[154] It is with good reason that the older and established Churches, committed to a new evangelization, have increased the numbers of their catechists and intensified catechetical activity. But "the term 'catechists' belongs above all to the catechists in mission lands ... Churches that are flourishing today would not have been built up without them".[155]

Even with the extension of the services rendered by lay people both within and outside the Church, there is always need for the ministry of catechists, a ministry with its own characteristics. Catechists are specialists, direct witnesses and irreplaceable evangelizers who, as I have often stated and experienced during my missionary journeys, represent the basic strength of Christian communities, especially in the young Churches. The new Code of Canon Law acknowledges the tasks, qualities and qualifications of catechists.[156]

However, it must not be forgotten that the work of catechists is becoming more and more difficult and demanding as a result of ecclesial

---

[154] SECOND VATICAN ECUMENICAL COUNCIL, Decree on the Missionary Activity of the Church *Ad Gentes,* 17.
[155] Apostolic Exhortation *Catechesi Tradendae,* 66: *loc. cit.,* 1331.
[156] Cf. c. 785, 1.

and cultural changes. What the Council suggested is still valid today: a more careful doctrinal and pedagogical training, continuing spiritual and apostolic renewal, and the need to provide "a decent standard of living and social security".[157] It is also important to make efforts to establish and support schools for catechists, which are to be approved by the Episcopal Conferences and confer diplomas officially recognized by the latter.[158]

74. Besides catechists, mention must also be made of other ways of serving the Church and her mission; namely, other Church personnel: leaders of prayer, song and liturgy; leaders of basic ecclesial communities and Bible study groups; those in charge of charitable works; administrators of Church resources; leaders in the various forms of the apostolate; religion teachers in schools. All the members of the laity ought to devote a part of their time to the Church, living their faith authentically.

---

[157] Decree on the Missionary Activity of the Church *Ad Gentes*, 17.

[158] Cf. Plenary Assembly of the Sacred Congregation for the Evangelization of Peoples, 1969, on catechists, and the related "Instruction" of April 1970: *Bibliographia Missionaria* 34 (1970), 197-212 and *S. C. de Propaganda Fide Memoria Rerum*, III/2 (1976), 821-831.

THE CONGREGATION
FOR THE EVANGELIZATION OF PEOPLES
AND OTHER STRUCTURES
FOR MISSIONARY ACTIVITY

75. Leaders and agents of missionary pastoral activity should sense their unity within the communion which characterizes the Mystical Body. Christ prayed for this at the Last Supper when he said: "Even as you, Father are in me, and I in you, that they also may be in us, so that the world may believe that you have sent me" (*Jn* 17:21). The fruitfulness of missionary activity is to be found in this communion.

But since the Church is also a communion which is visible and organic, her mission requires an external and ordered union between the various responsibilities and functions involved, in such a way that all the members "may in harmony spend their energies for the building up of the Church".[159]

To the Congregation responsible for missionary activity it falls "to direct and coordinate throughout the world the work of evangelizing peoples and of missionary cooperation, with due regard for the competence of the Congregation for the Oriental Churches".[160] Hence, its task is to "recruit missionaries and

---

[159] SECOND VATICAN ECUMENICAL COUNCIL, Decree on the Missionary Activity of the Church *Ad Gentes,* 28.

[160] Apostolic Constitution *Pastor Bonus* (28 June 1988), 85: *AAS* 80 (1988), 881; cf. SECOND VATICAN ECUMENICAL COUNCIL, Decree on the Missionary Activity of the Church *Ad Gentes,* 29.

distribute them in accordance with the more urgent needs of various regions ... draw up an ordered plan of action, issue norms and directives, as well as principles which are appropriate for the work of evangelization, and assist in the initial stages of their work".[161] I can only confirm these wise directives. In order to re-launch the mission *ad gentes,* a centre of outreach, direction and coordination is needed, namely, the Congregation for the Evangelization of Peoples. I invite the Episcopal Conferences and their various bodies, the Major Superiors of Orders, Congregations and Institutes, as well as lay organizations involved in missionary activity, to cooperate faithfully with this Dicastery, which has the authority necessary to plan and direct missionary activity and cooperation worldwide.

The same Congregation, which has behind it a long and illustrious history, is called to play a role of primary importance with regard to reflection and programmes of action which the Church needs in order to be more decisively oriented towards the mission in its various forms. To this end, the Congregation should maintain close relations with the other Dicasteries of the Holy See, with the local Churches and the various missionary forces. In an ecclesiology of communion in which the entire Church is missionary, but in which

<hr>

[161] SECOND VATICAN ECUMENICAL COUNCIL, Decree on the Missionary Activity of the Church *Ad Gentes,* 29: Cf. JOHN PAUL II, Apostolic Constitution *Pastor Bonus,* 86: *loc. cit.,* 882.

specific vocations and institutions for missionary work *ad gentes* remain indispensable, the guiding and coordinating role of the Congregation for the Evangelization of Peoples remains very important in order to ensure a united effort in confronting great questions of common concern, with due regard for the competence proper to each authority and structure.

76. Episcopal Conferences and their various groupings have great importance in directing and coordinating missionary activity on the national and regional levels. The Council asks them to "confer together in dealing with more important questions and urgent problems, without, however, overlooking local differences",[162] and to consider the complex issue of inculturation. In fact, large-scale and regular activity is already taking place in this area, with visible results. It is an activity which must be intensified and better coordinated with that of other bodies of the same Conferences, so that missionary concern will not be left to the care of only one sector or body, but will be shared by all.

The bodies and institutions involved in missionary activity should join forces and initiatives as opportunity suggests. Conferences of Major Superiors should have this same concern in their own sphere, maintaining

---

[162] Decree on the Missionary Activity of the Church *Ad Gentes*, 31.

contact with Episcopal Conferences in accordance with established directives and norms,[163] and also having recourse to mixed commissions.[164] Also desirable are meetings and other forms of cooperation between the various missionary institutions, both in formation and study,[165] as well as in the actual apostolate.

[163] Cf. *ibid.*, 33.

[164] Cf. PAUL VI, Apostolic Letter Motu Proprio *Ecclesiae Sanctae* (6 August 1966), II, 43: *AAS* 58 (1966), 782.

[165] Cf. SECOND VATICAN ECUMENICAL COUNCIL, Decree on the Missionary Activity of the Church *Ad Gentes,* 34; PAUL VI, Apostolic Letter Motu Proprio *Ecclesiae Sanctae,* III, 22: *loc. cit.,* 787.

CHAPTER VII

COOPERATION
IN MISSIONARY ACTIVITY

77.   Since they are members of the Church
by virtue of their Baptism, all Christians share
responsibility for missionary activity. "Missionary cooperation" is the expression used to
describe the sharing by communities and individual Christians in this right and duty.

Missionary cooperation is rooted and lived,
above all, in personal union with Christ. Only
if we are united to him as the branches to the
vine (cf. *Jn* 15:5) can we produce good fruit.
Through holiness of life every Christian can
become a fruitful part of the Church's mission.
The Second Vatican Council invited all "to a
profound interior renewal, so that having a
lively awareness of their personal responsibility
for the spreading of the Gospel, they may
play their part in missionary work among the
nations".[166]

Sharing in the universal mission therefore
is not limited to certain specific activities, but

---

[166] SECOND VATICAN ECUMENICAL COUNCIL, Decree on
the Missionary Activity of the Church *Ad Gentes*, 35; cf. *CIC*,
cc. 211, 781.

is the sign of maturity in faith and of a Christian life that bears fruit. In this way, individual believers extend the reach of their charity and show concern for those both far and near. They pray for the missions and missionary vocations. They help missionaries and follow their work with interest. And when missionaries return, they welcome them with the same joy with which the first Christian communities heard from the Apostles the marvellous things which God had wrought through their preaching (cf. *Acts* 14:27).

PRAYER AND SACRIFICE FOR MISSIONARIES

78.   Among the forms of sharing, first place goes to spiritual cooperation through prayer, sacrifice and the witness of Christian life. Prayer should accompany the journey of missionaries so that the proclamation of the word will be effective through God's grace. In his Letters, Saint Paul often asks the faithful to pray for him so that he might proclaim the Gospel with confidence and conviction. Prayer needs to be accompanied by sacrifice. The redemptive value of suffering, accepted and offered to God with love, derives from the sacrifice of Christ himself, who calls the members of his Mystical Body to share in his sufferings, to complete them in their own flesh (cf. *Col* 1:24). The sacrifice of missionaries should be shared and accompanied by the sacrifices of all the faithful. I therefore urge those engaged in

the pastoral care of the sick to teach them about the efficacy of suffering, and to encourage them to offer their sufferings to God for missionaries. By making such an offering, the sick themselves become missionaries, as emphasized by a number of movements which have sprung up among them and for them. The Solemnity of Pentecost—the beginning of the Church's mission—is celebrated in some communities as a "Day of Suffering for the Missions".

"HERE I AM, LORD! I AM READY! SEND ME!" (cf. *Is* 6:8)

79. Cooperation is expressed above all by promoting missionary vocations. While acknowledging the validity of various ways of being involved in missionary activity, it is necessary at the same time to reaffirm that *a full and lifelong commitment to the work of the missions holds pride of place,* especially in missionary Institutes and Congregations. Promoting such vocations is at the heart of missionary cooperation. Preaching the Gospel requires preachers; the harvest needs labourers. The mission is carried out above all by men and women who are consecrated for life to the work of the Gospel and are prepared to go forth into the whole world to bring salvation.

I wish to call to mind and to recommend this *concern for missionary vocations.* Conscious of the overall responsibility of Christians to contribute to missionary activity and to the development of poorer peoples, we must ask ourselves how it is that in some countries, while monetary contributions are on the increase, missionary vocations, which are the real measure of self-giving to one's brothers and sisters, are in danger of disappearing. Vocations to the priesthood and the consecrated life are a sure sign of the vitality of a Church.

80. As I think of this serious problem, I appeal with great confidence and affection to families and to young people. Families, especially parents, should be conscious that they ought to "offer a special contribution to the missionary cause of the Church by fostering missionary vocations among their sons and daughters". [167]

An intense prayer life, a genuine sense of service to one's neighbour and a generous participation in Church activities provide families with conditions that favour vocations among young people. When parents are ready to allow one of their children to leave for the missions, when they have sought this grace from the Lord, he will repay them, in joy, on the day that their son or daughter hears his call.

I ask young people themselves to listen to Christ's words as he says to them what he

---

[167] Apostolic Exhortation *Familiaris Consortio*, 54: *loc. cit.*, 147.

once said to Simon Peter and to Andrew at the lakeside: "Follow me, and I will make you fishers of men" (*Mt* 4:19). May they have the courage to reply as Isaiah did: "Here am I, Lord! I am ready! Send me!" (cf. *Is* 6:8). They will have a wonderful life ahead of them, and they will know the genuine joy of proclaiming the "Good News" to brothers and sisters whom they will lead on the way of salvation.

"IT IS MORE BLESSED TO GIVE THAN TO RECEIVE" (*Acts* 20:35)

81.   The material and financial needs of the missions are many: not only to set up the Church with minimal structures (chapels, schools for catechists and seminarians, housing), but also to support works of charity, education and human promotion—a vast field of action especially in poor countries. The missionary Church gives what she receives, and distributes to the poor the material goods that her materially richer sons and daughters generously put at her disposal. Here I wish to thank all those who make sacrifices and contribute to the work of the missions. Their sacrifices and sharing are indispensable for building up the Church and for showing love.

In the matter of material help, it is important to consider the spirit in which donations are made. For this we should reassess our own way of living: the missions ask not only for a contribution but for a sharing in the work of preaching and charity towards the poor. All that we have received from God—life itself as well as material goods—does not belong to us but is given to us for our use. Generosity in giving must always be enlightened and inspired by faith: then we will truly be more blessed in giving than in receiving.

World Mission Day, which seeks to heighten awareness of the missions, as well as to collect funds for them, is an important date in the life of the Church, because it teaches how to give: as an offering made to God, *in* the Eucharistic celebration and *for* all the missions of the world.

NEW FORMS OF MISSIONARY COOPERATION

82. Today, cooperation includes new forms—not only economic assistance, but also direct participation. New situations connected with the phenomenon of mobility demand from Christians an authentic missionary spirit.

International tourism has now become a mass phenomenon. This is a positive development if tourists maintain an attitude of respect and a desire for mutual cultural enrichment, avoiding ostentation and waste, and seeking contact with other people. But Christians are expected above all to be aware of their obligation to bear witness always to their faith and love of Christ. Firsthand knowledge of the missionary life and of new Christian communities also can be an enriching experience and can strengthen one's faith. Visiting the missions is commendable, especially on the part of young people who go there to serve and to gain an intense experience of the Christian life.

Reasons of work nowadays bring many Christians from young communities to areas where Christianity is unknown and at times prohibited or persecuted. The same is true of members of the faithful from traditionally Christian countries who work for a time in non-Christian countries. These circumstances are certainly an opportunity to live the faith and to bear witness to it. In the early centuries, Christianity spread because Christians, travelling to or settling in regions where Christ had not yet been proclaimed, bore courageous witness to their faith and founded the first communities there.

More numerous are the citizens of mission countries and followers of non-Christian religions who settle in other nations for reasons of study or work, or are forced to do so because of the political or economic situations in their native lands. The presence of these brothers and sisters in traditionally Christian countries is a challenge for the ecclesial communities, and a stimulus to hospitality, dialogue, service, sharing, witness and direct proclamation. In Christian countries, communities and cultural groups are also forming which call for the mission *ad gentes,* and the local Churches, with the help of personnel from the immigrants' own countries and of returning missionaries, should respond generously to these situations.

Missionary cooperation can also involve leaders in politics, economics, culture and journalism, as well as experts of the various international bodies. In the modern world it is becoming increasingly difficult to determine geographical or cultural boundaries. There is an increasing interdependence between peoples, and this constitutes a stimulus for Christian witness and evangelization.

MISSIONARY PROMOTION AND FORMATION AMONG THE PEOPLE OF GOD

83. Missionary formation is the task of the local Church, assisted by missionaries and their Institutes, and by personnel from the young Churches. This work must be seen not as peripheral but as central to the Christian life. Even for the "new evangelization" of Christian countries the theme of the missions can prove very helpful: the witness of missionaries retains its appeal even for the non-practising and non-believers, and it communicates Christian values. Particular Churches should therefore make the promotion of the missions a key element in the normal pastoral activity of parishes, associations and groups, especially youth groups.

With this end in view, it is necessary to spread information through missionary publications and audiovisual aids. These play an important role in making known the life of the universal Church and in voicing the experiences of missionaries and of the local Churches in which they work. In those younger Churches which are still not able to have a press and other means of their own, it is important that Missionary Institutes devote personnel and resources to these undertakings.

Such formation is entrusted to priests and their associates, to educators and teachers, and to theologians, particularly those who teach in seminaries and centres for the laity. Theological training cannot and should not ignore the Church's universal mission, ecumenism, the study of the great religions and missiology. I recommend that such studies be undertaken especially in seminaries and in houses of formation for men and women Religious, ensuring that some priests or other students specialize in the different fields of missiology.

Activities aimed at promoting interest in the missions must always be geared to these specific goals; namely, informing and forming the People of God to share in the Church's universal mission, promoting vocations *ad gentes* and encouraging cooperation in the work of evangelization. It is not right to give an incomplete picture of missionary activity, as if it consisted principally in helping the poor, contributing to the liberation of the oppressed, promoting development or defending human rights. The missionary Church is certainly involved on these fronts but her primary task lies elsewhere: the poor are hungry for God, not just for bread and freedom. Missionary activity must first of all bear witness to and proclaim salvation in Christ, and establish local Churches which then become means of liberation in every sense.

THE PRIMARY RESPONSIBILITY
OF THE *PONTIFICAL MISSION SOCIETIES*

84.   The leading role in this work of promotion belongs to the *Pontifical Mission Societies,* as I have often pointed out in my Messages for World Mission Day. The four Societies— Propagation of the Faith, Saint Peter the Apostle, Holy Childhood and the Missionary Union—have the common purpose of fostering a universal missionary spirit among the People of God. The Missionary Union has as its immediate and specific purpose the promotion of missionary consciousness and formation among priests and men and women Religious, who in turn will provide this consciousness and formation within the Christian communities. In addition, the Missionary Union seeks to promote the other Societies, of which it is the "soul". [168] "This must be our motto: All the

[168] Cf. PAUL VI, Apostolic Epistle *Graves et Increscentes* (5 September 1966): *AAS* 58 (1966), 750-756.

138

Churches united for the conversion of the whole world".[169]

Because they are under the auspices of the Pope and of the College of Bishops, these Societies, also within the boundaries of the particular Churches, rightly have "the first place ... since they are the means by which Catholics from their very infancy are imbued with a genuinely universal and missionary spirit; they are also the means which ensure an effective collection of resources for the good of all the missions, in accordance with the needs of each one".[170] Another purpose of the Missionary Societies is the fostering of lifelong vocations *ad gentes,* in both the older and younger Churches. I earnestly recommend that their promotional work be increasingly directed to this goal.

In their activities, these Societies depend at the worldwide level on the Congregation for the Evangelization of Peoples; at the local level they depend on the Episcopal Conferences and the Bishops of individual Churches, in collaboration with existing promotional centres. They bring to the Catholic world that spirit of universality and of service to the Church's mission, without which authentic cooperation does not exist.

[169] P. MANNA, *Le nostre "Chiese" e la propagazione del Vangelo,* Trentola Ducenta, 1952², p. 35.
[170] SECOND VATICAN ECUMENICAL COUNCIL, Decree on the Missionary Activity of the Church *Ad Gentes,* 38.

Not Only Giving to the Missions But Receiving From Them As Well

85. Cooperating in missionary activity means not just giving but also receiving. All the particular Churches, both young and old, are called to give and to receive in the context of the universal mission, and none should be closed to the needs of others. The Council states: "By virtue of ... catholicity, the individual parts bring their own gifts to the other parts and to the whole Church, in such a way that the whole and individual parts grow greater through the mutual communication of all and their united efforts towards fulness in unity ... Between the different parts of the Church there are bonds of intimate communion with regard to spiritual riches, apostolic workers and temporal assistance".[171]

I exhort all the Churches, and the Bishops, priests, religious and members of the laity, to *be open to the Church's universality,* and to avoid every form of provincialism or exclusiveness, or feelings of self-sufficiency. Local Churches, although rooted in their own people and their own culture, must always maintain an effective sense of the universality of the faith, giving and receiving spiritual gifts, experiences of pastoral work in evangelization and initial

---

[171] Dogmatic Constitution on the Church *Lumen Gentium,* 13.

proclamation, as well as personnel for the apostolate and material resources.

The temptation to become isolated can be a strong one. The older Churches, involved in new evangelization, may think that their mission is now at home, and thus they may risk slackening their drive towards the non-Christian world, begrudgingly conceding vocations to missionary Institutes, Religious Congregations or other particular Churches. But it is by giving generously of what we have that we will receive. Already the young Churches, many of which are blessed with an abundance of vocations, are in a position to send priests and men and women Religious to the older Churches.

On the other hand, the young Churches are concerned about their own identity, about inculturation, and about their freedom to grow independently of external influences, with the possible result that they close their doors to missionaries. To these Churches I say: Do not isolate yourselves; willingly accept missionaries and support from other Churches, and do likewise throughout the world. Precisely because of the problems that concern you, you need to be in continuous contact with your brothers and sisters in the faith. With every legitimate means, seek to ensure recognition of the freedom to which you have a right, remembering that Christ's disciples must "obey God rather than men" (*Acts* 5:29).

GOD IS PREPARING A NEW SPRINGTIME FOR THE GOSPEL

86.   If we look at today's world, we are struck by many negative factors that can lead to pessimism. But this feeling is unjustified: we have faith in God our Father and Lord, in his goodness and mercy. As the third Millennium of the Redemption draws near, God is preparing a great springtime for Christianity, and we can already see its first signs. In fact, both in the non-Christian world and in the traditionally Christian world, people are gradually drawing closer to Gospel ideals and values, a development which the Church seeks to encourage. Today in fact there is a new consensus among peoples about these values: the rejection of violence and war; respect for the human person and for human rights; the desire for freedom, justice and brotherhood; the surmounting of different forms of racism and nationalism; the affirmation of the dignity and role of women.

Christian hope sustains us in committing ourselves fully to the new evangelization and to the worldwide mission, and leads us to pray as Jesus taught us: "Thy Kingdom come. Thy will be done, on earth as it is in heaven" (*Mt* 6:10).

The number of those awaiting Christ is still immense: the human and cultural groups not yet reached by the Gospel, or for whom the Church is scarsely present, are so widespread as to require the uniting of all the Church's resources. As she prepares to celebrate the Jubilee of the year 2000, the whole Church is even more committed to a new missionary advent. We must increase our apostolic zeal to pass on to others the light and joy of the faith, and to this high ideal the whole People of God must be educated.

We cannot be content when we consider the millions of our brothers and sisters, who like us have been redeemed by the blood of Christ but who live in ignorance of the love of God. For each believer, as for the entire Church, the missionary task must remain foremost, for it concerns the eternal destiny of humanity and corresponds to God's mysterious and merciful plan.

Chapter VIII

MISSIONARY SPIRITUALITY

87.   Missionary activity demands a specific spirituality, which applies in particular to all those whom God has called to be missionaries.

Being Led by the Spirit

This spirituality is expressed first of all by a life of complete docility to the Spirit. It commits us to being moulded from within by the Spirit, so that we may become ever more like Christ. It is not possible to bear witness to Christ without reflecting his image, which is made alive in us by grace and the power of the Spirit. This docility then commits us to receive the gifts of fortitude and discernment, which are essential elements of missionary spirituality.

An example of this is found with the Apostles during the Master's public life. Despite their love for him and their generous response to his call, they proved to be incapable of understanding his words and reluctant to follow him along the path of suffering and humiliation. The Spirit transformed them

144

into courageous witnesses to Christ and enlightened heralds of his word. It was the Spirit himself who guided them along the difficult and new paths of mission.

Today, as in the past, that mission is difficult and complex, and demands the courage and light of the Spirit. We often experience the dramatic situation of the first Christian community, which witnessed unbelieving and hostile forces "gathered together against the Lord and his Anointed" (*Acts* 4:26). Now, as then, we must pray that God will grant us boldness in preaching the Gospel; we must ponder the mysterious ways of the Spirit and allow ourselves to be led by him into all the truth (cf. *Jn* 16:13).

Living the Mystery of Christ, "the One who was Sent"

88.   An essential characteristic of missionary spirituality is intimate communion with Christ. We cannot understand or carry out the mission unless we refer it to Christ as the one who was sent to evangelize. Saint Paul describes Christ's attitude: "Have this mind among yourselves, which is yours in Christ Jesus, who, though he was in the form of God, did not count equality with God a thing to be grasped, but emptied himself, taking the form of a servant, being born in the likeness of men. And being found in human form he humbled himself and

145

became obedient unto death, even death on a Cross" (*Phil* 2:5-8).

The mystery of the Incarnation and Redemption is thus described as a total self-emptying which leads Christ to experience fully the human condition and to accept totally the Father's plan. This is an emptying of self which is permeated by love and expresses love. The mission follows this same path and leads to the foot of the Cross.

The missionary is required to "renounce himself and everything that up to this point he considered as his own, and to make himself everything to everyone".[172] This he does by a poverty which sets him free for the Gospel, overcoming attachment to the people and things about him, so that he may become a brother to those to whom he is sent and thus bring them Christ the Saviour. This is the goal of missionary spirituality: "To the weak I became weak ...; I have become all things to all men, that I might by all means save some. I do it all for the sake of the Gospel ..." (*1 Cor* 9:22-23).

It is precisely because he is "sent" that the missionary experiences the consoling presence of Christ, who is with him at every moment of life—"Do not be afraid ... for I am with you" (*Acts* 18:9-10)—and who awaits him in the heart of every person.

---

[172] SECOND VATICAN ECUMENICAL COUNCIL, Decree on the Missionary Activity of the Church *Ad Gentes*, 24.

Loving the Church and Humanity As Jesus Did

89.   Missionary spirituality is also marked by apostolic charity, the charity of Christ who came "to gather into one the children of God who are scattered abroad" (*Jn* 11:52), of the Good Shepherd who knows his sheep, who searches them out and offers his life for them (cf. *Jn* 10). Those who have the missionary spirit feel Christ's burning love for souls, and love the Church as Christ did.

The missionary is urged on by "zeal for souls", a zeal inspired by Christ's own charity, which takes the form of concern, tenderness, compassion, openness, availability and interest in people's problems. Jesus' love is very deep: he who "knew what was in man" (*Jn* 2:25) loved everyone by offering them redemption and suffered when it was rejected.

The missionary is a person of charity. In order to proclaim to all his brothers and sisters that they are loved by God and are capable of loving, he must show love towards all, giving his life for his neighbour. The missionary is the "universal brother", bearing in himself the Church's spirit, her openness to and interest in all peoples and individuals, especially the least and poorest of his brethren. As such, he overcomes barriers and divisions of race, caste, or ideology. He is a sign of God's love in the world–a love without exclusion or partiality.

Finally, like Christ he must love the Church: "Christ loved the Church and gave himself up for her" (*Eph* 5:25). This love, even to the point of giving one's life, is a focal point for him. Only profound love for the Church can sustain the missionary's zeal. His daily pressure, as Saint Paul says, is "anxiety for all the Churches" (*2 Cor* 11:28). For every missionary "fidelity to Christ cannot be separated from fidelity to the Church".[173]

THE TRUE MISSIONARY IS THE SAINT

)0.   The call to mission derives, of its nature, from the call to holiness. A missionary is really such only if he commits himself to the way of holiness: "Holiness must be called a fundamental presupposition and an irreplaceable condition for everyone in fulfilling the mission of salvation in the Church".[174]

The universal call to holiness is closely linked to the *universal call to mission*. Every member of the faithful is called to holiness and to mission. This was the earnest desire of the Council, which hoped to be able "to enlighten all people with the brightness of Christ, which gleams over the face of the Church, by preaching the Gospel to every creature".[175]   The

---

[173] SECOND VATICAN ECUMENICAL COUNCIL, Decree on the Ministry and Life of Priests *Presbyterorum Ordinis*, 14.
[174] Apostolic Exhortation *Christifideles Laici*, 17: *loc. cit.*, 419.
[175] Dogmatic Constitution on the Church *Lumen Gentium*, 1.

148

Church's missionary spirituality is a journey towards holiness.

The renewed impulse to the mission *ad gentes* demands holy missionaries. It is not enough to update pastoral techniques, organize and co-ordinate ecclesial resources, or delve more deeply into the biblical and theological foundations of faith. What is needed is the encouragement of a new "ardour for holiness" among missionaries and throughout the Christian community, especially among those who work most closely with missionaries.[176]

Dear Brothers and Sisters: let us remember the missionary enthusiasm of the first Christian communities. Despite the limited means of travel and communication in those times, the proclamation of the Gospel quickly reached the ends of the earth. And this was the religion of a Man who had died on a cross, "a stumbling block to Jews and folly to Gentiles" (*1 Cor* 1:23)! Underlying this missionary dynamism was the holiness of the first Christians and the first communities.

91. I therefore address myself to the recently baptized members of the young communities and young Churches. Today, you are the hope of this two-thousand-year-old Church of ours: being young in faith, you must be like

---

[176] Cf. *Address* at CELAM Meeting, Port-au-Prince, 9 March 1983: *AAS* 75 (1983), 771-779; *Homily* for the Opening of the "Novena of Years" promoted by CELAM, Santo Domingo, 12 October 1984: *Insegnamenti* VII/2 (1984), 885-897.

the first Christians and radiate enthusiasm and courage, in generous devotion to God and neighbour. In a word, you must set yourselves on the path of holiness. Only thus can you be a sign of God in the world and re-live in your own countries the missionary epic of the early Church. You will also be a leaven of missionary spirit for the older Churches.

For their part, missionaries should reflect on the duty of holiness required of them by the gift of their vocation, renew themselves in spirit day by day, and strive to update their doctrinal and pastoral formation. The missionary must be a "contemplative in action". He finds answers to problems in the light of God's word and in personal and community prayer. My contact with representatives of the non-Christian spiritual traditions, particularly those of Asia, has confirmed me in the view that the future of mission depends to a great extent on contemplation. Unless the missionary is a contemplative he cannot proclaim Christ in a credible way. He is a witness to the experience of God, and must be able to say with the Apostles: "that which we have looked upon ... concerning the word of life, ... we proclaim also to you" (1 Jn 1:1-3).

The missionary is a person of the Beatitudes. Before sending out the Twelve to evangelize, Jesus, in his "missionary discourse" (cf. Mt 10), teaches them the paths of mission: poverty, meekness, acceptance of suffering and persecution, the desire for justice and peace,

150

charity—in other words, the Beatitudes, lived out in the apostolic life (cf. *Mt* 5, 1-12). By living the Beatitudes, the missionary experiences and shows concretely that the Kingdom of God has already come, and that he has accepted it. The characteristic of every authentic missionary life is the inner joy that comes from faith. In a world tormented and oppressed by so many problems, a world tempted to pessimism, the one who proclaims the "Good News" must be a person who has found true hope in Christ.

CONCLUSION

92.   Today, as never before, the Church has
the opportunity of bringing the Gospel, by
witness and word, to all people and nations. I
see the dawning of a new missionary age,
which will become a radiant day bearing an
abundant harvest, if all Christians, and missionaries and young Churches in particular,
respond with generosity and holiness to the
calls and challenges of our time.

Like the Apostles after Christ's Ascension,
the Church must gather in the Upper Room
"together with Mary the Mother of Jesus"
(*Acts* 1:14), in order to pray for the Spirit and
to gain strength and courage to carry out the
missionary mandate. We too, like the Apostles,
need to be transformed and guided by the
Spirit.

On the eve of the third Millennium the
whole Church is invited to live more intensely
the mystery of Christ by gratefully cooperating
in the work of salvation. The Church does this
together with Mary and following the example
of Mary, the Church's Mother and model:
Mary is the model of that maternal love
which should inspire all who cooperate in the
Church's apostolic mission for the rebirth of

humanity. Therefore, "strengthened by the presence of Christ, the Church journeys through time towards the consummation of the ages and goes to meet the Lord who comes. But on this journey ... she proceeds along *the path* already trodden by the Virgin Mary".[177]

To "Mary's mediation, wholly oriented towards Christ and tending to the revelation of his salvific power",[178] I entrust the Church and, in particular, those who commit themselves to carrying out the missionary mandate in today's world. As Christ sent forth his Apostles in the name of the Father and of the Son and of the Holy Spirit, so too, renewing that same mandate, I extend to all of you my Apostolic Blessing, in the name of the same Most Holy Trinity. Amen.

Given in Rome, at Saint Peter's, on 7 December, the Twenty-fifth Anniversary of the Conciliar Decree *Ad Gentes,* in the year 1990, the thirteenth of my Pontificate.

Joannes Paulus PP. II

---

[177] Encyclical Letter *Redemptoris Mater* (25 March 1987), 2: *AAS* 79 (1987), 362f.
[178] *Ibid.,* 22: *loc. cit.,* 390.